YOUR PERSONAL
HOROSCOPE
2010

LIBRA

YOUR PERSONAL HOROSCOPE 2010

LIBRA
24th September–23rd October

igloo

igloo

This edition published by Igloo Books Ltd,
Cottage Farm, Sywell, Northants NN6 0BJ
www.igloo-books.com

Produced for Igloo Books by W. Foulsham & Co. Ltd,
The Oriel, Thames Valley Court, 183–187 Bath Road, Slough,
Berkshire SL1 4AA, England

ISBN: 978-1-84817-693-5

This is an abridged version of material
originally published in *Old Moore's Horoscope
and Astral Diary*.

Printed and manufactured in China

CONTENTS

INTRODUCTION

Your Personal Horoscopes have been specifically created to allow you to get the most from astrological patterns and the way they have a bearing on not only your zodiac sign, but nuances within it. Using the diary section of the book you can read about the influences and possibilities of each and every day of the year. It will be possible for you to see when you are likely to be cheerful and happy or those times when your nature is in retreat and you will be more circumspect. The diary will help to give you a feel for the specific 'cycles' of astrology and the way they can subtly change your day-to-day life. For example, when you see the sign ☿, this means that the planet Mercury is retrograde at that time. Retrograde means it appears to be running backwards through the zodiac. Such a happening has a significant effect on communication skills, but this is only one small aspect of how the Personal Horoscope can help you.

With Your Personal Horoscope the story doesn't end with the diary pages. It includes simple ways for you to work out the zodiac sign the Moon occupied at the time of your birth, and what this means for your personality. In addition, if you know the time of day you were born, it is possible to discover your Ascendant, yet another important guide to your personal make-up and potential.

Many readers are interested in relationships and in knowing how well they get on with people of other astrological signs. You might also be interested in the way you appear to very different sorts of individuals. If you are such a person, the section on Venus will be of particular interest. Despite the rapidly changing position of this planet, you can work out your Venus sign, and learn what bearing it will have on your life.

Using Your Personal Horoscope you can travel on one of the most fascinating and rewarding journeys that anyone can take – the journey to a better realisation of self.

7

THE ESSENCE OF LIBRA

Exploring the Personality of Libra the Scales

(24TH SEPTEMBER – 23RD OCTOBER)

What's in a sign?

At heart you may be the least complicated of all the zodiac sign types, though your ruling element is Air, and that is always going to supply some surprises. Diplomatic, kind and affectionate, your nature blows like a refreshing breeze through the lives of almost anyone you meet. It isn't like you to be gloomy for very long at a time, and you know how to influence the world around you.

It's true that you don't like dirt, or too much disorganisation, and you tend to be very artistic by inclination. You get your own way in life, not by dint of making yourself unpopular in any way but rather with the sort of gentle persuasion to which almost everyone you know falls victim at one time or another. Being considerate of others is more or less second nature to you, though you may not be quite as self-sacrificing as sometimes appears to be the case. You definitely know what you want from life and are not above using a little subterfuge when it comes to getting it.

You are capable and resourceful, but just a little timid on occasions. All the same, when dealing with subject matter that you know and relish, few can better you out there in the practical world. You know how to order your life and can be just as successful in a career sense as you tend to be in your home life. There are times when personal attractions can be something of a stumbling block because you love readily and are very influenced by the kindness and compliments of those around you.

Librans do need to plan ahead, but don't worry about this fact too much because you are also extremely good at thinking on your feet. Getting others to do your bidding is a piece of cake because you are not tardy when it comes to showing your affections. Nevertheless you need to be careful not to allow yourself to fall into unreliable company, or to get involved in schemes that seem too good to be true – some of them are. But for most of the time you present a happy picture to the world and get along just fine, with your ready smile and adaptable personality. You leave almost any situation happier and more contented than it was when you arrived.

Libra resources

When it comes to getting on in life you have as much ammunition in your armoury as most zodiac signs and a great deal more than some. For starters you are adaptable and very resourceful. When you have to take a leap in logic there is nothing preventing you from doing so, and the strong intuition of which your zodiac sign is capable can prove to be very useful at times.

One of your strongest points is the way you manage to make others love you. Although you might consider yourself to be distinctly 'ordinary', that's not the way the world at large perceives you. Most Librans have the ability to etch themselves onto the minds of practically everyone they come across. Why? It's simple. You listen to what people have to say and appear to be deeply interested. On most occasions you are, but even if the tale is a tedious one you give the impression of being rooted to the spot with a determination to hear the story right through. When it comes to responding you are extremely diplomatic and always manage to steer a sensible course between any two or more opposing factions.

Having said that you don't like dirt or untidy places, this is another fact that you can turn to your advantage, because you can always find someone who will help you out. So charming can Libra be that those who do all they can to make you more comfortable regularly end up feeling that you have done them a favour.

It is the sheer magic of the understated Libran that does the trick every time. Even on those rare occasions when you go out with all guns blazing to get what you want from life, you are very unlikely to make enemies on the way. Of course you do have to be careful on occasions, like everyone, but you can certainly push issues further than most. Why? Mainly because people don't realise that you are doing so.

You could easily sell any commodity – though it might be necessary to believe in it yourself first. Since you can always see the good points in anything and tend to be generally optimistic, that should not be too problematical either.

Beneath the surface

In many respects Libra could be the least complicated sign of the zodiac so it might be assumed that 'what you see is what you get'. Life is rarely quite that simple, though you are one of the most straightforward people when it comes to inner struggle. The fact is that most Librans simply don't have a great deal. Between subconscious motivation and in-your-face action there is a seamless process. Librans do need to be loved and this fact can be quite a strong motivation in itself towards any particular course of action. However, even this desire for affection isn't the most powerful factor when considering the sign of the Scales.

What matters most to you is balance, which is probably not at all surprising considering what your zodiac sign actually means. Because of this you would go to tremendous lengths to make sure that your inner resolves create the right external signs and actions to offer the peace that you are looking for most of all.

Like most people born under the Air signs you are not quite as confident as you sometimes appear to be. In the main you are modest and not given to boasting, so you don't attract quite the level of attention of your fellow Air signs, Gemini and Aquarius. All the same you are quite capable of putting on an act when it's necessary to give a good account of yourself in public. You could be quaking inside but you do have the ability to hide this from the world at large.

Librans exhibit such a strong desire to be kind to everyone they meet that they may hide their inner feelings from some people altogether. It's important to remember to be basically honest, even if that means upsetting others a little. This is the most difficult trait for Libra to deal with and may go part of the way to explaining why so many relationship break-ups occur for people born under this zodiac sign. However, as long as you find ways and means to explain your deepest emotional needs, at least to those you love, all should be well.

In most respects you tend to be an open book, particularly to those who take the trouble to look. Your nature is not over-deep, and you are almost certainly not on some secret search to find the 'real you'. Although Libra is sometimes accused of being superficial there are many people in the world who would prefer simplicity to complications and duplicity.

Making the best of yourself

This may be the easiest category by far for the zodiac sign of Libra. The fact is that you rarely do anything else but offer the best version of what you are. Presentation is second nature to Libra, which just loves to be noticed. Despite this you are naturally modest and so not inclined to go over the top in company. You can be relied upon to say and do the right things for most of the time. Even when you consider your actions to be zany and perhaps less acceptable, this is not going to be the impression that the majority of people would get.

In a work sense you need to be involved in some sort of occupation that is clean, allows for a sense of order and ultimately offers the ability to use your head as well as your hands. The fact is that you don't care too much for unsavoury sorts of work and need to be in an environment that suits your basically refined nature. If the circumstances are right you can give a great deal to your work and will go far. Librans also need to be involved with others because they are natural co-operators. For this reason you may not be at your best when working alone or in situations that necessitate all the responsibilities being exclusively yours.

When in the social mainstream you tend to make the best of yourself by simply being what you naturally are. You don't need frills and fancies. Libra is able to make the best sort of impression by using the natural qualities inherent in the sign. As a result, your natural poise, your ability to cut through social divisions, your intelligence and your adaptability should all ensure that you remain popular.

What may occasionally prove difficult is being quite as dominant as the world assumes you ought to be. Many people equate efficiency with power. This is not the way of people born under the Scales, and you need to make that fact plain to anyone who seems to have the desire to shape you.

The impressions you give

Although the adage 'what you see is what you get' may be truer for Libra than for any of its companion signs, it can't be exclusively the case. However, under almost all circumstances you are likely to make friends. You are a much shrewder operator than sometimes appears to be the case and tend to weigh things in the balance very carefully. Libra can be most things to most people, and that's the sort of adaptability that ensures success at both a social and a professional level.

The chances are that you are already well respected and deeply liked by most of the people you know. This isn't so surprising since you are not inclined to make waves of any sort. Whether or not this leads to you achieving the degree of overall success that you deserve in life is quite a different matter. When impressions count you don't tend to let yourself down, or the people who rely on you. Adapting yourself to suit different circumstances is the meat and drink of your basic nature and you have plenty of poise and charm to disarm even the most awkward of people.

In affairs of the heart you are equally adept at putting others at their ease. There is very little difficulty involved in getting people to show their affection for you and when it comes to romance you are one of the most successful practitioners to be found anywhere. The only slight problem in this area of life, as with others, is that you are so talented at offering people what they want that you might not always be living the sort of life that genuinely suits you. Maybe giving the right impression is a little too important for Libra. A deeper form of honesty from the start would prevent you from having to show a less charming side to your nature in the end.

In most circumstances you can be relied upon to exhibit a warm, affectionate, kind, sincere and interesting face to the world at large. As long as this underpins truthfulness it's hard to understand how Libra could really go far wrong.

The way forward

You must already be fairly confident that you have the necessary skills and natural abilities to get on well in a world that is also filled with other people. From infancy most Librans learn how to rub along with others, whilst offering every indication that they are both adaptable and amenable to change. Your chameleon-like ability to 'change colour' in order to suit prevailing circumstances means that you occasionally drop back to being part of the wallpaper in the estimation of at least some people. A greater ability to make an impression probably would not go amiss sometimes, but making a big fuss isn't your way and you actively seek an uncomplicated sort of life.

Balance is everything to Libra, a fact that means there are times when you end up with nothing at all. What needs to be remembered is that there are occasions when everyone simply has to make a decision. This is the hardest thing in the world for you to do but when you manage it you become even more noticed by the world at large.

There's no doubt that people generally hold you in great affection. They know you to be quite capable and love your easy-going attitude to life. You are rarely judgmental and tend to offer almost anyone the benefit of the doubt. Although you are chatty, and inclined to listen avidly to gossip, it isn't your natural way to be unkind, caustic or backbiting. As a result it would seem that you have all the prerequisites to live an extremely happy life. Alas, things are rarely quite that easy.

It is very important for you to demonstrate to yourself, as well as to others, that you are an individual with thoughts and feelings of your own. So often do you defer to the needs of those around you that the real you gets somewhat squashed on the way. There have to be times when you are willing to say 'yes' or 'no' unequivocally, instead of a noncommittal 'I don't really mind' or 'whatever you think best'. At the end of the day you do have opinions and can lead yourself into the path of some severe frustrations if you are unwilling to voice them in the first place.

Try to be particularly honest in deep, emotional attachments. Many Libran relationships come to grief simply because there isn't enough earthy honesty present in the first place. People knowing how you feel won't make them care for you any less. A fully integrated, truthful Libran, with a willingness to participate in the decision making, turns out to be the person who is both successful and happy.

LIBRA ON THE CUSP

Astrological profiles are altered for those people born at either the beginning or the end of a zodiac sign, or, more properly, on the cusps of a sign. In the case of Libra this would be on the 24th of September and for two or three days after, and similarly at the end of the sign, probably from the 21st to the 23rd of October.

The Virgo Cusp – September 24th to 26th

Here we find a Libran subject with a greater than average sense of responsibility and probably a better potential for success than is usually the case for Libra when taken alone. The Virgoan tendency to take itself rather too seriously is far less likely when the sign is mixed with Libra and the resultant nature is often deeply inspiring, and yet quite centred. The Virgo-cusp Libran has what it takes to break through the red tape of society, and yet can understand the need for its existence in the first place. You are caring and concerned, quick on the uptake and very ready to listen to any point of view but, at the end of the day, you know when it is going to be necessary to take a personal stance and this you are far more willing to do than would be the case for non-cuspid Librans.

Family members are important to you, but you always allow them their own individuality and won't get in the way of their personal need to spread their own wings, even at times when it's hard to take this positive stance. Practically speaking, you are a good home-maker but you also enjoy travelling and can benefit greatly from seeing the way other cultures think and behave. It is true that you can have the single- mindedness of a Virgoan, but even this aspect is modified by the Libran within you, so that you usually try to see alternative points of view and often succeed in doing so.

At work you really come into your own. Not only are you capable enough to deal with just about any eventuality, you are also willing to be flexible and to make up your mind instantly when it proves necessary to do so. Colleagues and subordinates alike tend to trust you. You may consider self-employment, unlike most Librans who are usually very worried by this prospect. Making your way in life is something you tend to take for granted, even when the going gets tough.

What people most like about you is that, despite your tremendously practical approach to life, you can be very zany and retain a sense of fun that is, at its best, second to none. Few people find you difficult to understand or to get on with in a day-to-day sense.

The Scorpio Cusp – October 21st to 23rd

The main difference between this cusp and the one at the Virgo end of Libra, is that you tend to be more emotionally motivated and of a slightly less practical nature. Routines are easy for you to address, though you can become very restless and tend to find your own emotional responses difficult to deal with. Sometimes even you don't understand what makes you tick, and that can be a problem. Actually you are not as complicated as you may have come to believe. It's simply that you have a unique view of life and one that doesn't always match that of the people around you, but as Libra instinctively wants to conform, this can lead to some personal confusion.

In family matters you are responsible, very caring and deeply committed to others. It's probable that you work in some field that finds you in direct contact with the public at large and many Scorpio-cusp Librans choose welfare, social or hospital work as a first choice. When it comes to love, you are flexible in your choice and the necessary attributes to promote a long-lasting and happy relationship are clearly present in your basic nature. If there are problems, they may come about as a result of your inability to choose properly in the first place, because you are the first to offer anyone the benefit of the doubt.

When it comes to the practicalities of life, Scorpio can prove to be extremely useful. It offers an 'edge' to your nature and, as Scorpio is a Fixed sign, you are less likely to lose ground because of lack of confidence than Libra alone would be. Your future can be bright, but only if you are willing to get involved in something that really interests you in the first place. You certainly do not care for getting your hands dirty and tend to gravitate towards more refined positions.

Creative potential is good and you could be very artistic, though if this extends to fine art, at least some of your pictures will have 'dark' overtones that might shock some people, including yourself. At base you are kind, caring, complicated, yet inspiring.

LIBRA AND ITS
ASCENDANTS

The nature of every individual on the planet is composed of the rich variety of zodiac signs and planetary positions that were present at the time of their birth. Your Sun sign, which in your case is Libra, is one of the many factors when it comes to assessing the unique person you are. Probably the most important consideration, other than your Sun sign, is to establish the zodiac sign that was rising over the eastern horizon at the time that you were born. This is your Ascending or Rising sign. Most popular astrology fails to take account of the Ascendant, and yet its importance remains with you from the very moment of your birth, through every day of your life. The Ascendant is evident in the way you approach the world, and so, when meeting a person for the first time, it is this astrological influence that you are most likely to notice first. Our Ascending sign essentially represents what we appear to be, while the Sun sign is what we feel inside ourselves.

The Ascendant also has the potential for modifying our overall nature. For example, if you were born at a time of day when Libra was passing over the eastern horizon (this would be around the time of dawn) then you would be classed as a double Libran. As such, you would typify this zodiac sign, both internally and in your dealings with others. However, if your Ascendant sign turned out to be a Water sign, such as Pisces, there would be a profound alteration of nature, away from the expected qualities of Libra.

One of the reasons why popular astrology often ignores the Ascendant is that it has always been rather difficult to establish. We have found a way to make this possible by devising an easy-to-use table, which you will find on page 157 of this book. Using this, you can establish your Ascendant sign at a glance. You will need to know your rough time of birth, then it is simply a case of following the instructions.

For those readers who have no idea of their time of birth it might be worth allowing a good friend, or perhaps your partner, to read through the section that follows this introduction. Someone who deals with you on a regular basis may easily discover your Ascending sign, even though you could have some difficulty establishing it for yourself. A good understanding of this component of your nature is essential if you want to be aware of that 'other person' who is responsible for the way you make contact with the world at large. Your Sun sign, Ascendant sign, and the other pointers in this book will, together, allow you a far better understanding of what makes you tick as an individual. Peeling back the different layers of your astrological make-up can be an enlightening experience, and the Ascendant may represent one of the most important layers of all.

Libra with Libra Ascendant

There is no doubt that you carry the very best of all Libran worlds in your nature, though at the same time there is a definite possibility that you often fall between two stools. The literal advice as a result is that you must sometimes make a decision, even though it isn't all that easy for you to do so. Not everyone understands your easy-going side and there are occasions when you could appear to be too flippant for your own good.

The way you approach the world makes you popular, and there is no doubt at all that you are the most diplomatic person to be found anywhere in the length and breadth of the zodiac. It is your job in life to stop people disagreeing and since you can always see every point of view, you make a good impression on the way.

Relationships can sometimes be awkward for you because you can change your mind so easily. But love is never lacking and you can be fairly certain of a generally happy life. Over-indulging is always a potential problem for Air-sign people such as yourself, and there are times in your life when you must get the rest and relaxation which is so important in funding a strong nervous system. Drink plenty of water to flush out a system that can be over-high in natural salts.

Libra with Scorpio Ascendant

There is some tendency for you to be far more deep than the average Libran would appear to be, and for this reason it is crucial that you lighten up from time to time. Every person with a Scorpio quality needs to remember that there is a happy and carefree side to all events, and your Libran quality should allow you to bear this in mind. Sometimes you try to do too many things at the same time. This is fine if you take the casual overview of Libra, but less sensible when you insist on picking the last bone out of every potential, as is much more the case for Scorpio.

When worries come along, as they sometimes will, be able to listen to what your friends have to say and also realise that they are more than willing to work on your behalf, if only because you are so loyal to them. You do have a quality of self-deception, but this should not get in the way too much if you combine the instinctive actions of Libra with the deep intuition of your Scorpio component.

Probably the most important factor of this combination is your ability to succeed in a financial sense. You make a good manager, but not of the authoritarian sort. Jobs in the media or where you are expected to make up your mind quickly would suit you because there is always an underpinning of practical sense that rarely lets you down.

Libra with Sagittarius Ascendant

A very happy combination this, with a great desire for life in all its forms and a need to push forward the bounds of the possible in a way that few other zodiac sign connections would do. You don't like the unpleasant or ugly in life and yet you are capable of dealing with both if you have to. Giving so much to humanity, you still manage to retain a degree of individuality that would surprise many, charm others, and please all.

On the reverse side of the same coin you might find that you are sometimes accused of being fickle, but this is only an expression of your need for change and variety, which is endemic to both these signs. True, you have more of a temper than would be the case for Libra when taken on its own, but such incidents would see you up and down in a flash, and it is almost impossible for you to bear a grudge of any sort. Routines get on your nerves and you are far happier when you can please yourself and get ahead at your own pace, which is quite fast.

As a lover you can make a big impression and most of you will not go short of affection in the early days, before you choose to commit yourself. Once you do, there is always a chance of romantic problems, but these are less likely when you have chosen carefully in the first place.

Libra with Capricorn Ascendant

It is a fact that Libra is the most patient of the Air signs, though like the others it needs to get things done fairly quickly. Capricorn, on the other hand, will work long and hard to achieve its objectives and will not be thwarted in the end. As a result this is a quite powerful sign combination and one that should lead to ultimate success.

Capricorn is often accused of taking itself too seriously and yet it has an ironic and really very funny sense of humour which only its chief confidants recognise. Libra is lighthearted, always willing to have fun and quite anxious to please. When these two basic types come together in their best forms, you might find yourself to be one of the most well-balanced people around. Certainly you know what you want, but you don't have to use a bulldozer in order to get it.

Active and enthusiastic when something really takes your fancy, you might also turn out to be one of the very best lovers of them all. The reason for this is that you have the depth of Capricorn but the lighter and more directly affectionate qualities of the Scales. What you want from life in a personal sense, you eventually tend to get, but you don't care too much if this takes you a while. Few people could deny that you are a faithful friend, a happy sort and a deeply magnetic personality.

Libra with Aquarius Ascendant

Stand by for a truly interesting and very inspiring combination here, but one that is sometimes rather difficult to fathom, even for the sort of people who believe themselves to be very perceptive. The reason for this could be that any situation has to be essentially fixed and constant in order to get a handle on it, and this is certainly not the case for the Aquarian–Libran type. The fact is that both these signs are Air signs, and to a certain extent as unpredictable as the wind itself.

To most people you seem to be original, frank, free and very outspoken. Not everything you do makes sense to others, and if you were alive during the hippy era, it is likely that you went around with flowers in your hair, for you are a free-thinking idealist at heart. With age you mature somewhat, but never too much, because you will always see the strange, the comical and the original in life. This is what keeps you young and is one of the factors that makes you so very attractive to members of the opposite sex. Many people will want to 'adopt' you, and you are at your very best when in company.

Much of your effort is expounded on others and yet, unless you discipline yourself a good deal, personal relationships of the romantic sort can bring certain difficulties. Careful planning is necessary.

Libra with Pisces Ascendant

An Air and Water combination, you are not easy to understand and have depths that show at times, surprising those people who thought they already knew what you were. You will always keep people guessing and are just as likely to hitchhike around Europe as you are to hold down a steady job, both of which you would undertake with the same degree of commitment and success. Usually young at heart, but always carrying the potential for an old head on young shoulders, you are something of a paradox and not at all easy for totally 'straight' types to understand. But you always make an impression and tend to be very attractive to members of the opposite sex.

In matters of health you do have to be a little careful because you dissipate much nervous energy and can sometimes be inclined to push yourself too hard, at least in a mental sense. Frequent periods of rest and meditation will do you the world of good and should improve your level of wisdom, which tends to be fairly high already. Much of your effort in life is expounded on behalf of humanity as a whole, for you care deeply, love totally and always give of your best. Whatever your faults and failings might be, you are one of the most popular people around.

Libra with Aries Ascendant

Libra has the tendency to bring out the best in any zodiac sign, and this is no exception when it comes together with Aries. You may, in fact, be the most comfortable of all Aries types, simply because Libra tempers some of your more assertive qualities and gives you the chance to balance out opposing forces, both inside yourself and in the world outside. You are fun to be with and make the staunchest friend possible. Although you are generally affable, few people would try to put one over on you because they would quickly come to know how far you are willing to go before you let forth a string of invective that would shock those who previously underestimated your basic Aries traits.

Home and family are very dear to you, but you are more tolerant than some Aries types are inclined to be and you have a youthful zest for life that should stay with you no matter what age you manage to achieve. There is always something interesting to do and your mind is a constant stream of possibilities. This makes you very creative and you may also demonstrate a desire to look good at all times. You may not always be quite as confident as you appear to be, but few would guess the fact.

Libra with Taurus Ascendant

A fortunate combination in many ways, this is a double-Venus rulership, since both Taurus and Libra are heavily reliant on the planet of love. You are social, amiable and a natural diplomat, anxious to please and ready to care for just about anyone who shows interest in you. You hate disorder, which means that there is a place for everything and everything in its place. This can throw up the odd paradox however, since being half Libran you cannot always work out where that place ought to be! You deal with life in a humorous way and are quite capable of seeing the absurd in yourself, as well as in others. Your heart is no bigger than that of the quite typical Taurean, but it sits rather closer to the surface and so others recognise it more.

On those occasions when you know you are standing on firm ground you can show great confidence, even if you have to be ready to change some of your opinions at the drop of a hat. When this happens you can be quite at odds with yourself, because Taurus doesn't take very many U-turns, whereas Libra does. Don't expect to know yourself too well, and keep looking for the funny side of things, because it is within humour that you forge the sort of life that suits you best.

Libra with Gemini Ascendant

What a happy-go-lucky soul you are and how popular you tend to be with those around you. Libra is, like Gemini, an Air sign and this means that you are the communicator par excellence, even by Gemini standards. It can sometimes be difficult for you to make up your mind about things because Libra does not exactly aid this process, and especially not when it is allied to Mercurial Gemini. Frequent periods of deep thought are necessary, and meditation would do you a great deal of good. All the same, although you might sometimes be rather unsure of yourself, you are rarely without a certain balance. Clean and tidy surroundings suit you the best, though this is far from easy to achieve because you are invariably dashing off to some place or other, so you really need someone to sort things out in your absence.

The most important fact of all is that you are much loved by your friends, of which there are likely to be very many. Because you are so willing to help them out, in return they are usually there when it matters and they would probably go to almost any length on your behalf. You exhibit a fine sense of justice and will usually back those in trouble. Charities tend to be attractive to you and you do much on behalf of those who live on the fringes of society or people who are truly alone.

LIBRA AND ITS ASCENDANTS

Libra with Cancer Ascendant

What an absolutely pleasant and approachable sort of person you are, and how much you have to offer. Like most people associated with the sign of Cancer you give yourself freely to the world, and will always be on hand if anyone is in trouble or needs the special touch you can bring to almost any problem. Behaving in this way is the biggest part of what you are and so people come to rely on you very heavily. Like Libra you can see both sides of any coin and you exhibit the Libran tendency to jump about from one foot to the other when it is necessary to make decisions relating to your own life. This is not usually the case when you are dealing with others however, because the cooler and more detached qualities of Cancer will show through in these circumstances.

It would be fair to say that you do not deal with routines as well as Cancer alone might do and you need a degree of variety in your life, which in your case often comes in the form of travel, which can be distant and of long duration. It isn't unusual for people who have this zodiac combination to end up living abroad, though even this does little to prevent you from getting itchy feet from time to time. In romance you show an original quality that keeps the relationship young and working very well.

Libra with Leo Ascendant

Libra brings slightly more flexibility to the fixed quality of the Leo nature. On the whole you do not represent a picture that is so much different from other versions of the Lion, though you find more time to smile, enjoy changing your mind a great deal more and have a greater number of casual friends. Few would find you proud or haughty and you retain the common touch that can be so important when it comes to getting on in life generally. At work you like to do something that brings variety, and would probably soon tire of doing the same task over and over again. Many of you are teachers, for you have patience, allied to a stubborn core. This can be an indispensable combination on occasions and is part of the reason for the material success that many folk with this combination of signs achieve.

It isn't often that you get down in the dumps, after all there is generally something more important around the next corner, and you love the cut and thrust of everyday life. You always manage to stay young at heart, no matter what your age might be, and you revel in the company of interesting and stimulating types. Maybe you should try harder to concentrate on one thing at once and also strive to retain a serious opinion for more than ten minutes at a time. However, Leo helps to control your flighty tendencies.

Libra with Virgo Ascendant

Libra has the ability to lighten almost any load, and it is particularly good at doing so when it is brought together with the much more repressed sign of Virgo. To the world at large you seem relaxed, happy and able to cope with most of the pressures that life places upon you. Not only do you deal with your own life in a bright and breezy manner but you are usually on hand to help others out of any dilemma that they might make for themselves. With excellent powers of communication, you leave the world at large in no doubt whatsoever concerning both your opinions and your wishes. It is in the talking stakes that you really excel because Virgo brings the silver tongue of Mercury and Libra adds the Air-sign desire to be in constant touch with the world outside your door.

You like to have a good time and can often be found in the company of interesting and stimulating people, who have the ability to bring out the very best in your bright and sparkling personality. Underneath however, there is still much of the worrying Virgoan to be found and this means that you have to learn to relax inside as well as appearing to do so externally. In fact you are much more complex than most people would realise, and definitely would not be suited to a life that allowed you too much time to think about yourself.

THE MOON AND THE PART IT PLAYS IN YOUR LIFE

In astrology the Moon is probably the single most important heavenly body after the Sun. Its unique position, as partner to the Earth on its journey around the solar system, means that the Moon appears to pass through the signs of the zodiac extremely quickly. The zodiac position of the Moon at the time of your birth plays a great part in personal character and is especially significant in the build-up of your emotional nature.

Your Own Moon Sign

Discovering the position of the Moon at the time of your birth has always been notoriously difficult because tracking the complex zodiac positions of the Moon is not easy. This process has been reduced to three simple stages with our Lunar Tables. A breakdown of the Moon's zodiac positions can be found from page 35 onwards, so that once you know what your Moon Sign is, you can see what part this plays in the overall build-up of your personal character.

If you follow the instructions on the next page you will soon be able to work out exactly what zodiac sign the Moon occupied on the day that you were born and you can then go on to compare the reading for this position with those of your Sun sign and your Ascendant. It is partly the comparison between these three important positions that goes towards making you the unique individual you are.

HOW TO DISCOVER YOUR MOON SIGN

This is a three-stage process. You may need a pen and a piece of paper but if you follow the instructions below the process should only take a minute or so.

STAGE 1 First of all you need to know the Moon Age at the time of your birth. If you look at Moon Table 1, on page 33, you will find all the years between 1912 and 2010 down the left side. Find the year of your birth and then trace across to the right to the month of your birth. Where the two intersect you will find a number. This is the date of the New Moon in the month that you were born. You now need to count forward the number of days between the New Moon and your own birthday. For example, if the New Moon in the month of your birth was shown as being the 6th and you were born on the 20th, your Moon Age Day would be 14. If the New Moon in the month of your birth came after your birthday, you need to count forward from the New Moon in the previous month. Whatever the result, jot this number down so that you do not forget it.

STAGE 2 Take a look at Moon Table 2 on page 34. Down the left hand column look for the date of your birth. Now trace across to the month of your birth. Where the two meet you will find a letter. Copy this letter down alongside your Moon Age Day.

STAGE 3 Moon Table 3 on page 34 will supply you with the zodiac sign the Moon occupied on the day of your birth. Look for your Moon Age Day down the left hand column and then for the letter you found in Stage 2. Where the two converge you will find a zodiac sign and this is the sign occupied by the Moon on the day that you were born.

Your Zodiac Moon Sign Explained

You will find a profile of all zodiac Moon Signs on pages 35 to 38, showing in yet another way how astrology helps to make you into the individual that you are. In each daily entry of the Astral Diary you can find the zodiac position of the Moon for every day of the year. This also allows you to discover your lunar birthdays. Since the Moon passes through all the signs of the zodiac in about a month, you can expect something like twelve lunar birthdays each year. At these times you are likely to be emotionally steady and able to make the sort of decisions that have real, lasting value.

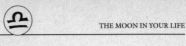

MOON TABLE 1

YEAR	AUG	SEP	OCT	YEAR	AUG	SEP	OCT	YEAR	AUG	SEP	OCT
1912	13	12	11	1945	8	6	6	1978	4	2	2/31
1913	2/31	30	29	1946	26	25	24	1979	22	21	20
1914	21	19	19	1947	16	14	14	1980	11	10	9
1915	10	9	8	1948	5	3	2	1981	29	28	27
1916	29	27	27	1949	24	23	21	1982	19	17	17
1917	17	15	15	1950	13	12	11	1983	8	7	6
1918	6	4	4	1951	2	1	1/30	1984	26	25	24
1919	25	23	23	1952	20	19	18	1985	16	14	14
1920	14	12	12	1953	9	8	8	1986	5	4	3
1921	3	2	1/30	1954	28	27	26	1987	24	23	22
1922	22	21	20	1955	17	16	15	1988	12	11	10
1923	12	10	10	1956	6	4	4	1989	1/31	29	29
1924	30	28	28	1957	25	23	23	1990	20	19	18
1925	19	18	17	1958	15	13	12	1991	9	8	8
1926	8	7	6	1959	4	3	2/31	1992	28	26	25
1927	27	25	25	1960	22	21	20	1993	17	16	15
1928	16	14	14	1961	11	10	9	1994	7	5	5
1929	5	3	2	1962	30	28	28	1995	26	24	24
1930	24	22	20	1963	19	17	17	1996	14	13	11
1931	13	12	11	1964	7	6	5	1997	3	2	2/31
1932	2/31	30	29	1965	26	25	24	1998	22	20	20
1933	21	19	19	1966	16	14	14	1999	11	10	8
1934	10	9	8	1967	5	4	3	2000	29	27	27
1935	29	27	27	1968	24	23	22	2001	19	17	17
1936	17	15	15	1969	12	11	10	2002	8	6	6
1937	6	4	4	1970	2	1	1/30	2003	27	26	25
1938	25	23	23	1971	20	19	19	2004	14	13	12
1939	15	13	12	1972	9	8	8	2005	4	3	2
1940	4	2	1/30	1973	28	27	26	2006	23	22	21
1941	22	21	20	1974	17	16	15	2007	13	12	11
1942	12	10	10	1975	7	5	5	2008	1/31	30	29
1943	1/30	29	29	1976	25	23	23	2009	20	19	18
1944	18	17	17	1977	14	13	12	2010	10	8	8

TABLE 2   MOON TABLE 3

DAY	SEP	OCT	M/D	X	Y	Z	a	b	d	e
1	X	a	0	VI	VI	LI	LI	LI	LI	SC
2	X	a	1	VI	LI	LI	LI	LI	SC	SC
3	X	a	2	LI	LI	LI	LI	SC	SC	SC
4	Y	b	3	LI	LI	SC	SC	SC	SC	SA
5	Y	b	4	LI	SC	SC	SC	SA	SA	SA
6	Y	b	5	SC	SC	SC	SA	SA	SA	CP
7	Y	b	6	SC	SA	SA	SA	CP	CP	CP
8	Y	b	7	SA	SA	SA	SA	CP	CP	AQ
9	Y	b	8	SA	SA	CP	CP	CP	CP	AQ
10	Y	b	9	SA	CP	CP	CP	AQ	AQ	AQ
11	Y	b	10	CP	CP	CP	AQ	AQ	AQ	PI
12	Y	b	11	CP	AQ	AQ	AQ	PI	PI	PI
13	Y	b	12	AQ	AQ	AQ	PI	PI	PI	AR
14	Z	d	13	AQ	AQ	PI	PI	AR	PI	AR
15	Z	d	14	PI	PI	PI	AR	AR	AR	TA
16	Z	d	15	PI	PI	PI	AR	AR	AR	TA
17	Z	d	16	PI	AR	AR	AR	AR	TA	TA
18	Z	d	17	AR	AR	AR	AR	TA	TA	GE
19	Z	d	18	AR	AR	AR	TA	TA	GE	GE
20	Z	d	19	AR	TA	TA	TA	TA	GE	GE
21	Z	d	20	TA	TA	TA	GE	GE	GE	CA
22	Z	d	21	TA	GE	GE	GE	GE	CA	CA
23	Z	d	22	GE	GE	GE	GE	CA	CA	CA
24	a	e	23	GE	GE	GE	CA	CA	CA	LE
25	a	e	24	GE	CA	CA	CA	CA	LE	LE
26	a	e	25	CA	CA	CA	CA	LE	LE	LE
27	a	e	26	CA	LE	LE	LE	LE	VI	VI
28	a	e	27	LE	LE	LE	LE	VI	VI	VI
29	a	e	28	LE	LE	LE	VI	VI	VI	LI
30	a	e	29	LE	VI	VI	VI	VI	LI	LI
31	–	e								

AR = Aries, TA = Taurus, GE = Gemini, CA = Cancer, LE = Leo, VI = Virgo,
LI = Libra, SC = Scorpio, SA = Sagittarius, CP = Capricorn, AQ = Aquarius, PI = Pisces

MOON SIGNS

Moon in Aries

You have a strong imagination, courage, determination and a desire to do things in your own way and forge your own path through life.

Originality is a key attribute; you are seldom stuck for ideas although your mind is changeable and you could take the time to focus on individual tasks. Often quick-tempered, you take orders from few people and live life at a fast pace. Avoid health problems by taking regular time out for rest and relaxation.

Emotionally, it is important that you talk to those you are closest to and work out your true feelings. Once you discover that people are there to help, there is less necessity for you to do everything yourself.

Moon in Taurus

The Moon in Taurus gives you a courteous and friendly manner, which means you are likely to have many friends.

The good things in life mean a lot to you, as Taurus is an Earth sign that delights in experiences which please the senses. Hence you are probably a lover of good food and drink, which may in turn mean you need to keep an eye on the bathroom scales, especially as looking good is also important to you.

Emotionally you are fairly stable and you stick by your own standards. Taureans do not respond well to change. Intuition also plays an important part in your life.

Moon in Gemini

You have a warm-hearted character, sympathetic and eager to help others. At times reserved, you can also be articulate and chatty: this is part of the paradox of Gemini, which always brings duplicity to the nature. You are interested in current affairs, have a good intellect, and are good company and likely to have many friends. Most of your friends have a high opinion of you and would be ready to defend you should the need arise. However, this is usually unnecessary, as you are quite capable of defending yourself in any verbal confrontation.

Travel is important to your inquisitive mind and you find intellectual stimulus in mixing with people from different cultures. You also gain much from reading, writing and the arts but you do need plenty of rest and relaxation in order to avoid fatigue.

Moon in Cancer

The Moon in Cancer at the time of birth is a fortunate position as Cancer is the Moon's natural home. This means that the qualities of compassion and understanding given by the Moon are especially enhanced in your nature, and you are friendly and sociable and cope well with emotional pressures. You cherish home and family life, and happily do the domestic tasks. Your surroundings are important to you and you hate squalor and filth. You are likely to have a love of music and poetry.

Your basic character, although at times changeable like the Moon itself, depends on symmetry. You aim to make your surroundings comfortable and harmonious, for yourself and those close to you.

Moon in Leo

The best qualities of the Moon and Leo come together to make you warm-hearted, fair, ambitious and self-confident. With good organisational abilities, you invariably rise to a position of responsibility in your chosen career. This is fortunate as you don't enjoy being an 'also-ran' and would rather be an important part of a small organisation than a menial in a large one.

You should be lucky in love, and happy, provided you put in the effort to make a comfortable home for yourself and those close to you. It is likely that you will have a love of pleasure, sport, music and literature. Life brings you many rewards, most of them as a direct result of your own efforts, although you may be luckier than average and ready to make the best of any situation.

Moon in Virgo

You are endowed with good mental abilities and a keen receptive memory, but you are never ostentatious or pretentious. Naturally quite reserved, you still have many friends, especially of the opposite sex. Marital relationships must be discussed carefully and worked at so that they remain harmonious, as personal attachments can be a problem if you do not give them your full attention.

Talented and persevering, you possess artistic qualities and are a good homemaker. Earning your honours through genuine merit, you work long and hard towards your objectives but show little pride in your achievements. Many short journeys will be undertaken in your life.

Moon in Libra

With the Moon in Libra you are naturally popular and make friends easily. People like you, probably more than you realise, you bring fun to a party and are a natural diplomat. For all its good points, Libra is not the most stable of astrological signs and, as a result, your emotions can be a little unstable too. Therefore, although the Moon in Libra is said to be good for love and marriage, your Sun sign and Rising sign will have an important effect on your emotional and loving qualities.

You must remember to relate to others in your decision-making. Co-operation is crucial because Libra represents the 'balance' of life that can only be achieved through harmonious relationships. Conformity is not easy for you because Libra, an Air sign, likes its independence.

Moon in Scorpio

Some people might call you pushy. In fact, all you really want to do is to live life to the full and protect yourself and your family from the pressures of life. Take care to avoid giving the impression of being sarcastic or impulsive and use your energies wisely and constructively.

You have great courage and you invariably achieve your goals by force of personality and sheer effort. You are fond of mystery and are good at predicting the outcome of situations and events. Travel experiences can be beneficial to you.

You may experience problems if you do not take time to examine your motives in a relationship, and also if you allow jealousy, always a feature of Scorpio, to cloud your judgement.

Moon in Sagittarius

The Moon in Sagittarius helps to make you a generous individual with humanitarian qualities and a kind heart. Restlessness may be intrinsic as your mind is seldom still. Perhaps because of this, you have a need for change that could lead you to several major moves during your adult life. You are not afraid to stand your ground when you know your judgement is right, you speak directly and have good intuition.

At work you are quick, efficient and versatile and so you make an ideal employee. You need work to be intellectually demanding and do not enjoy tedious routines.

In relationships, you anger quickly if faced with stupidity or deception, though you are just as quick to forgive and forget. Emotionally, there are times when your heart rules your head.

Moon in Capricorn

The Moon in Capricorn makes you popular and likely to come into the public eye in some way. The watery Moon is not entirely comfortable in the Earth sign of Capricorn and this may lead to some difficulties in the early years of life. An initial lack of creative ability and indecision must be overcome before the true qualities of patience and perseverance inherent in Capricorn can show through.

You have good administrative ability and are a capable worker, and if you are careful you can accumulate wealth. But you must be cautious and take professional advice in partnerships, as you are open to deception. You may be interested in social or welfare work, which suit your organisational skills and sympathy for others.

Moon in Aquarius

The Moon in Aquarius makes you an active and agreeable person with a friendly, easy-going nature. Sympathetic to the needs of others, you flourish in a laid-back atmosphere. You are broad-minded, fair and open to suggestion, although sometimes you have an unconventional quality which others can find hard to understand.

You are interested in the strange and curious, and in old articles and places. You enjoy trips to these places and gain much from them. Political, scientific and educational work interests you and you might choose a career in science or technology.

Money-wise, you make gains through innovation and concentration and Lunar Aquarians often tackle more than one job at a time. In love you are kind and honest.

Moon in Pisces

You have a kind, sympathetic nature, somewhat retiring at times, but you always take account of others' feelings and help when you can.

Personal relationships may be problematic, but as life goes on you can learn from your experiences and develop a better understanding of yourself and the world around you.

You have a fondness for travel, appreciate beauty and harmony and hate disorder and strife. You may be fond of literature and would make a good writer or speaker yourself. You have a creative imagination and may come across as an incurable romantic. You have strong intuition, maybe bordering on a mediumistic quality, which sets you apart from the mass. You may not be rich in cash terms, but your personal gifts are worth more than gold.

LIBRA IN LOVE

Discover how compatible you are with people from the same and other signs of the zodiac. Five stars equals a match made in heaven!

Libra meets Libra

This is a potentially successful match because Librans are extremely likeable people, and so it stands to reason that two Librans together will be twice as pleasant and twice as much fun. However, Librans can also be indecisive and need an anchor from which to find practical and financial success, and obviously one Libran won't provide this for another. Librans can be flighty in a romantic sense, so both parties will need to develop a steadfast approach for a long-term relationship. Star rating: ****

Libra meets Scorpio

Many astrologers have reservations about this match because, on the surface, the signs are so different. However, this couple may find fulfilment because these differences mean that their respective needs are met. Scorpio needs a partner to lighten the load which won't daunt Libra, while Libra looks for a steadfast quality which it doesn't possess, but Scorpio can supply naturally. Financial success is possible because they both have good ideas and back them up with hard work and determination. All in all, a promising outlook. Star rating: ****

Libra meets Sagittarius

Libra and Sagittarius are both adaptable signs who get on well with most people, but this promising outlook often does not follow through because each brings out the flighty side of the other. This combination is great for a fling, but when the romance is over someone needs to see to the practical side of life. Both signs are well meaning, pleasant and kind, but are either of them constant enough to build a life together? In at least some of the cases, the answer would be no. Star rating: ***

Libra meets Capricorn

Libra and Capricorn rub each other up the wrong way because their attitudes to life are so different, and although both are capable of doing something about this, in reality they probably won't. Capricorn is steady, determined and solid, while Libra is bright but sometimes superficial and not entirely reliable. They usually lack the instant spark needed to get them together in the first place, so when it does happen it is often because one of the partners is not typical of their sign. Star rating: **

Libra meets Aquarius

One of the best combinations imaginable, partly because both are Air signs and so share a common meeting point. But perhaps the more crucial factor is that both signs respect each other. Aquarius loves life and originality, and is quite intellectual. Libra is similar, but more balanced and rather less eccentric. A visit to this couple's house would be entertaining and full of zany wit, activity and excitement. Both are keen to travel and may prefer to 'find themselves' before taking on too many domestic responsibilities. Star rating: *****

Libra meets Pisces

Libra and Pisces can be extremely fond of each other, even deeply in love, but this alone isn't a stable foundation for long-term success. Pisces is extremely deep and doesn't even know itself very well. Libra may initially find this intriguing but will eventually feel frustrated at being unable to understand the Piscean's emotional and personal feelings. Pisces can be jealous and may find Libra's flightiness difficult, which Libra can't stand. They are great friends and they may make it to the romantic stakes, but when they get there a lot of effort will be necessary. Star rating: ***

Libra meets Aries

These are zodiac opposites which means a make-or-break situation. The match will either be a great success or a dismal failure. Why? Well, Aries finds it difficult to understand the flighty Air-sign tendencies of Libra, whilst the natural balance of Libra contradicts the unorthodox Arian methods. Any flexibility will come from Libra, which may mean that things work out for a while, but Libra only has so much patience and it may eventually run out. In the end, Aries may be just too bossy for an independent but sensitive sign like Libra. Star rating: **

Libra meets Taurus

A happy life is important to both these signs and, as they are both ruled by Venus, they share a common understanding, even though they display themselves so differently. Taurus is quieter than Libra, but can be decisive, and that's what counts. Libra is interested in absolutely everything, an infectious quality when seen through Taurean eyes. The slightly flighty qualities of Libra may lead to jealousy from the Bull. Not an argumentative relationship and one that often works well. There could be many changes of address for this pair. Star rating: ****

Libra meets Gemini

One of the best possible zodiac combinations. Libra and Gemini are both Air signs, which leads to a meeting of minds. Both signs simply love to have a good time, although Libra is the tidiest and less forgetful. Gemini's capricious nature won't bother Libra, who acts as a stabilising influence. Life should generally run smoothly, and any rows are likely to be short and sharp. Both parties genuinely like each other, which is of paramount importance in a relationship and, ultimately, there isn't a better reason for being or staying together. Star rating: *****

Libra meets Cancer

Almost anyone can get on with Libra, which is one of the most adaptable signs of them all. But being adaptable does not always lead to fulfilment and a successful match here will require a quiet Libran and a slightly more progressive Cancerian than the norm. Both signs are pleasant and polite, and like domestic order, but Libra may find Cancer too emotional and perhaps lacking in vibrancy, while Libra, on the other hand, may be a little too flighty for steady Cancer. Star rating: ***

Libra meets Leo

The biggest drawback here is likely to be in the issue of commitment. Leo knows everything about constancy and faithfulness, a lesson which, sadly, Libra needs to learn. Librans are easy-going and diplomatic, qualities which are useful when Leo is on the war-path. This couple should be compatible on a personal level and any problems tend to relate to the different way in which these signs deal with outside factors. With good will and an open mind, it can work out well enough. Star rating: ***

Libra meets Virgo

There have been some rare occasions when this match has found great success, but usually the darker and more inward-looking Virgoan depresses the naturally gregarious Libran. Libra appears self-confident, but is not so beneath the surface, and needs encouragement to develop inner confidence, which may not come from Virgo. Constancy can be a problem for Libra, who also tires easily and may find Virgo dull. A lighter, less serious approach to life from Virgo is needed to make this work. Star rating: **

VENUS:
THE PLANET OF LOVE

If you look up at the sky around sunset or sunrise you will often see Venus in close attendance to the Sun. It is arguably one of the most beautiful sights of all and there is little wonder that historically it became associated with the goddess of love. But although Venus does play an important part in the way you view love and in the way others see you romantically, this is only one of the spheres of influence that it enjoys in your overall character.

Venus has a part to play in the more cultured side of your life and has much to do with your appreciation of art, literature, music and general creativity. Even the way you look is responsive to the part of the zodiac that Venus occupied at the start of your life, though this fact is also down to your Sun sign and Ascending sign. If, at the time you were born, Venus occupied one of the more gregarious zodiac signs, you will be more likely to wear your heart on your sleeve, as well as to be more attracted to entertainment, social gatherings and good company. If on the other hand Venus occupied a quiet zodiac sign at the time of your birth, you would tend to be more retiring and less willing to shine in public situations.

It's good to know what part the planet Venus plays in your life for it can have a great bearing on the way you appear to the rest of the world and since we all have to mix with others, you can learn to make the very best of what Venus has to offer you.

One of the great complications in the past has always been trying to establish exactly what zodiac position Venus enjoyed when you were born because the planet is notoriously difficult to track. However, we have solved that problem by creating a table that is exclusive to your Sun sign, which you will find on the following page.

Establishing your Venus sign could not be easier. Just look up the year of your birth on the next page and you will see a sign of the zodiac. This was the sign that Venus occupied in the period covered by your sign in that year. If Venus occupied more than one sign during the period, this is indicated by the date on which the sign changed, and the name of the new sign. For instance, if you were born in 1950, Venus was in Virgo until the 4th October, after which time it was in Libra. If you were born before 4th October your Venus sign is Virgo, if you were born on or after 4th October, your Venus sign is Libra. Once you have established the position of Venus at the time of your birth, you can then look in the pages which follow to see how this has a bearing on your life as a whole.

1912 LIBRA / 30.9 SCORPIO
1913 LEO / 27.9 VIRGO /
    21.10 LIBRA
1914 SCORPIO / 10.10 SAGITTARIUS
1915 LIBRA / 16.10 SCORPIO
1916 LEO / 8.10 VIRGO
1917 SCORPIO / 12.10 SAGITTARIUS
1918 VIRGO / 6.10 LIBRA
1919 SCORPIO / 12.10 SAGITTARIUS
1920 LIBRA / 30.9 SCORPIO
1921 LEO / 26.9 VIRGO /
    21.10 LIBRA
1922 SCORPIO / 11.10 SAGITTARIUS
1923 LIBRA / 16.10 SCORPIO
1924 LEO / 8.10 VIRGO
1925 SCORPIO / 12.10 SAGITTARIUS
1926 VIRGO / 6.10 LIBRA
1927 VIRGO
1928 LIBRA / 29.9 SCORPIO
1929 LEO / 26.9 VIRGO /
    20.10 LIBRA
1930 SCORPIO / 12.10 SAGITTARIUS
1931 LIBRA / 15.10 SCORPIO
1932 LEO / 7.10 VIRGO
1933 SCORPIO / 11.10 SAGITTARIUS
1934 VIRGO / 5.10 LIBRA
1935 VIRGO
1936 LIBRA / 28.9 SCORPIO
1937 LEO / 25.9 VIRGO /
    20.10 LIBRA
1938 SCORPIO / 14.10 SAGITTARIUS
1939 LIBRA / 14.10 SCORPIO
1940 LEO / 7.10 VIRGO
1941 SCORPIO / 11.10 SAGITTARIUS
1942 VIRGO / 5.10 LIBRA
1943 VIRGO
1944 LIBRA / 28.9 SCORPIO
1945 LEO / 25.9 VIRGO /
    19.10 LIBRA
1946 SCORPIO / 14.10 SAGITTARIUS
1947 LIBRA / 13.10 SCORPIO
1948 LEO / 7.10 VIRGO
1949 SCORPIO / 11.10 SAGITTARIUS
1950 VIRGO / 4.10 LIBRA
1951 VIRGO
1952 LIBRA / 27.9 SCORPIO
1953 VIRGO / 19.10 LIBRA
1954 SCORPIO / 16.10 SAGITTARIUS
1955 LIBRA / 12.10 SCORPIO
1956 LEO / 6.10 VIRGO
1957 SCORPIO / 10.10 SAGITTARIUS
1958 VIRGO / 4.10 LIBRA

1959 VIRGO / 28.9 LEO
1960 LIBRA / 27.9 SCORPIO
1961 VIRGO / 18.10 LIBRA
1962 SCORPIO / 16.10 SAGITTARIUS
1963 LIBRA / 12.10 SCORPIO
1964 LEO / 6.10 VIRGO
1965 SCORPIO / 9.10 SAGITTARIUS
1966 VIRGO / 4.10 LIBRA
1967 VIRGO / 3.10 LEO
1968 LIBRA / 26.9 SCORPIO
1969 VIRGO / 17.10 LIBRA
1970 SCORPIO / 19.10 SAGITTARIUS
1971 LIBRA / 11.10 SCORPIO
1972 LEO / 6.10 VIRGO
1973 SCORPIO / 10.10 SAGITTARIUS
1974 VIRGO / 3.10 LIBRA
1975 VIRGO / 5.10 LEO
1976 LIBRA / 26.9 SCORPIO
1977 VIRGO / 17.10 LIBRA
1978 SCORPIO / 19.10 SAGITTARIUS
1979 LIBRA / 11.10 SCORPIO
1980 LEO / 5.10 VIRGO
1981 SCORPIO / 9.10 SAGITTARIUS
1982 VIRGO / 3.10 LIBRA
1983 VIRGO / 7.10 LEO
1984 LIBRA / 25.9 SCORPIO
1985 VIRGO / 16.10 LIBRA
1986 SCORPIO
1987 LIBRA / 10.10 SCORPIO
1988 LEO / 5.10 VIRGO
1989 SCORPIO / 8.10 SAGITTARIUS
1990 VIRGO / 2.10 LIBRA
1991 VIRGO / 8.10 LEO
1992 LIBRA / 25.9 SCORPIO
1993 VIRGO / 16.10 LIBRA
1994 SCORPIO
1995 LIBRA / 10.10 SCORPIO
1996 LEO / 5.10 VIRGO
1997 SCORPIO / 8.10 SAGITTARIUS
1998 VIRGO / 2.10 LIBRA
1999 VIRGO / 9.10 LEO
2000 LIBRA / 25.9 SCORPIO
2001 LEO / 5.10 VIRGO
2002 SCORPIO / 8.10 SAGITTARIUS
2003 LIBRA / 10.10 SCORPIO
2004 LEO / 5.10 VIRGO
2005 SCORPIO / 8.10 SAGITTARIUS
2006 VIRGO / 2.10 LIBRA
2007 VIRGO / 9.10 LEO
2008 LIBRA / 25.9 SCORPIO
2009 LEO / 5.10 VIRGO
2010 SCORPIO / 8.10 SAGITTARIUS

VENUS THROUGH THE ZODIAC SIGNS

Venus in Aries

Amongst other things, the position of Venus in Aries indicates a fondness for travel, music and all creative pursuits. Your nature tends to be affectionate and you would try not to create confusion or difficulty for others if it could be avoided. Many people with this planetary position have a great love of the theatre, and mental stimulation is of the greatest importance. Early romantic attachments are common with Venus in Aries, so it is very important to establish a genuine sense of romantic continuity. Early marriage is not recommended, especially if it is based on sympathy. You may give your heart a little too readily on occasions.

Venus in Taurus

You are capable of very deep feelings and your emotions tend to last for a very long time. This makes you a trusting partner and lover, whose constancy is second to none. In life you are precise and careful and always try to do things the right way. Although this means an ordered life, which you are comfortable with, it can also lead you to be rather too fussy for your own good. Despite your pleasant nature, you are very fixed in your opinions and quite able to speak your mind. Others are attracted to you and historical astrologers always quoted this position of Venus as being very fortunate in terms of marriage. However, if you find yourself involved in a failed relationship, it could take you a long time to trust again.

Venus in Gemini

As with all associations related to Gemini, you tend to be quite versatile, anxious for change and intelligent in your dealings with the world at large. You may gain money from more than one source but you are equally good at spending it. There is an inference here that you are a good communicator, via either the written or the spoken word, and you love to be in the company of interesting people. Always on the look-out for culture, you may also be very fond of music, and love to indulge the curious and cultured side of your nature. In romance you tend to have more than one relationship and could find yourself associated with someone who has previously been a friend or even a distant relative.

Venus in Cancer

You often stay close to home because you are very fond of family and enjoy many of your most treasured moments when you are with those you love. Being naturally sympathetic, you will always do anything you can to support those around you, even people you hardly know at all. This charitable side of your nature is your most noticeable trait and is one of the reasons why others are naturally so fond of you. Being receptive and in some cases even psychic, you can see through to the soul of most of those with whom you come into contact. You may not commence too many romantic attachments but when you do give your heart, it tends to be unconditionally.

Venus in Leo

It must become quickly obvious to almost anyone you meet that you are kind, sympathetic and yet determined enough to stand up for anyone or anything that is truly important to you. Bright and sunny, you warm the world with your natural enthusiasm and would rarely do anything to hurt those around you, or at least not intentionally. In romance you are ardent and sincere, though some may find your style just a little overpowering. Gains come through your contacts with other people and this could be especially true with regard to romance, for love and money often come hand in hand for those who were born with Venus in Leo. People claim to understand you, though you are more complex than you seem.

Venus in Virgo

Your nature could well be fairly quiet no matter what your Sun sign might be, though this fact often manifests itself as an inner peace and would not prevent you from being basically sociable. Some delays and even the odd disappointment in love cannot be ruled out with this planetary position, though it's a fact that you will usually find the happiness you look for in the end. Catapulting yourself into romantic entanglements that you know to be rather ill-advised is not sensible, and it would be better to wait before you committed yourself exclusively to any one person. It is the essence of your nature to serve the world at large and through doing so it is possible that you will attract money at some stage in your life.

Venus in Libra

Venus is very comfortable in Libra and bestows upon those people who have this planetary position a particular sort of kindness that is easy to recognise. This is a very good position for all sorts of friendships and also for romantic attachments that usually bring much joy into your life. Few individuals with Venus in Libra would avoid marriage and since you are capable of great depths of love, it is likely that you will find a contented personal life. You like to mix with people of integrity and intelligence but don't take kindly to scruffy surroundings or work that means getting your hands too dirty. Careful speculation, good business dealings and money through marriage all seem fairly likely.

Venus in Scorpio

You are quite open and tend to spend money quite freely, even on those occasions when you don't have very much. Although your intentions are always good, there are times when you get yourself in to the odd scrape and this can be particularly true when it comes to romance, which you may come to late or from a rather unexpected direction. Certainly you have the power to be happy and to make others contented on the way, but you find the odd stumbling block on your journey through life and it could seem that you have to work harder than those around you. As a result of this, you gain a much deeper understanding of the true value of personal happiness than many people ever do, and are likely to achieve true contentment in the end.

Venus in Sagittarius

You are lighthearted, cheerful and always able to see the funny side of any situation. These facts enhance your popularity, which is especially high with members of the opposite sex. You should never have to look too far to find romantic interest in your life, though it is just possible that you might be too willing to commit yourself before you are certain that the person in question is right for you. Part of the problem here extends to other areas of life too. The fact is that you like variety in everything and so can tire of situations that fail to offer it. All the same, if you choose wisely and learn to understand your restless side, then great happiness can be yours.

Venus in Capricorn

The most notable trait that comes from Venus in this position is that it makes you trustworthy and able to take on all sorts of responsibilities in life. People are instinctively fond of you and love you all the more because you are always ready to help those who are in any form of need. Social and business popularity can be yours and there is a magnetic quality to your nature that is particularly attractive in a romantic sense. Anyone who wants a partner for a lover, a spouse and a good friend too would almost certainly look in your direction. Constancy is the hallmark of your nature and unfaithfulness would go right against the grain. You might sometimes be a little too trusting.

Venus in Aquarius

This location of Venus offers a fondness for travel and a desire to try out something new at every possible opportunity. You are extremely easy to get along with and tend to have many friends from varied backgrounds, classes and inclinations. You like to live a distinct sort of life and gain a great deal from moving about, both in a career sense and with regard to your home. It is not out of the question that you could form a romantic attachment to someone who comes from far away or be attracted to a person of a distinctly artistic and original nature. What you cannot stand is jealousy, for you have friends of both sexes and would want to keep things that way.

Venus in Pisces

The first thing people tend to notice about you is your wonderful, warm smile. Being very charitable by nature you will do anything to help others, even if you don't know them well. Much of your life may be spent sorting out situations for other people, but it is very important to feel that you are living for yourself too. In the main, you remain cheerful, and tend to be quite attractive to members of the opposite sex. Where romantic attachments are concerned, you could be drawn to people who are significantly older or younger than yourself or to someone with a unique career or point of view. It might be best for you to avoid marrying whilst you are still very young.

LIBRA:
2009 DIARY PAGES

October
2009

1 THURSDAY
Moon Age Day 12   Moon Sign Pisces

Trends now assist you to analyse and sort out practical details. These you can then make work in a smoothly functioning system. Although your intuition remains strong, it is the practical side of life that offers the best rewards today. On the first day of a new month, there is much to be said for getting cracking with a new project.

2 FRIDAY
Moon Age Day 13   Moon Sign Pisces

Some disagreements are possible in the professional sphere, but you should try to ensure that the same isn't the case in personal attachments. On the contrary, if you can give endless time to your partner or sweetheart, you can increase their appreciation of you simply by being what you naturally are. Looking good is important in social settings.

3 SATURDAY
Moon Age Day 14   Moon Sign Pisces

Even if you are very eager to advance, in one or two ways you might be fairly short-sighted at the moment. Be prepared to look at the bigger picture and avoid getting bogged down by irrelevant details or silly fears. If you need a little assistance there are bound to be people around who can be persuaded to do what they can to sort you out.

4 SUNDAY
Moon Age Day 15   Moon Sign Aries

The lunar low heralds a tendency to do things in the most complicated and time-wasting manner. Ask yourself whether any of the tasks you intend to take on today could easily wait until you are more in the mood for them. Instead of working too much, why not take time out to relax and spend a few hours with the people you love?

5 MONDAY
Moon Age Day 16   Moon Sign Aries

If you have allowed jobs to mount up, dealing with a backlog at this point in time may be something of a challenge. The presence of the lunar low does little to assist your efforts, though as the day advances its influence should become less and less potent. If you concentrate on one thing at once you might even be able to ignore it altogether.

6 TUESDAY
Moon Age Day 17   Moon Sign Taurus

There isn't much doubt that you can afford to be ambitious at the moment. If there is something you particularly want, this is the time to go for it, and with some strong supporting planetary influences you can get most things to fall into place. Make the most of any chances later in the day to show your partner how you really feel about them.

7 WEDNESDAY
Moon Age Day 18   Moon Sign Taurus

By all means rely on your instincts today, because they are unlikely to let you down. If you feel just a little sluggish, this could be because you are not getting as much exercise as you should or that you are failing to take time out to do what pleases you. Why not ring the changes in some way and get together with like-minded friends if you can?

8 THURSDAY
Moon Age Day 19   Moon Sign Gemini

You express yourself best today by constantly projecting your ego. Even if being big-headed or bragging about your accomplishments isn't your style, everyone needs to feel proud of themselves sometimes. Gaining the approval of friends can help you to raise your self-esteem. The evening brings an opportunity to seek affection.

9 FRIDAY
Moon Age Day 20   Moon Sign Gemini

You are now entering a truly expansive phase and a time when you can increase the influence of your ideas. Trends encourage you to take advantage of the wise counsel and sensible decisions of others, maybe family members, and when it comes to giving the best of impressions socially, you have what it takes to be right on the ball.

51

10 SATURDAY   *Moon Age Day 21   Moon Sign Gemini*

Capitalise on enthusiasm for new career plans, perhaps by spending at least part of the weekend sorting things out. In addition, the social side of your nature is to the fore, so there are good reasons for getting together with those whose ideas about life mirror your own. A day to keep busy and to get tedious jobs out of the way in a flash.

11 SUNDAY   *Moon Age Day 22   Moon Sign Cancer*

It may well benefit you to be slightly pushier than you have been recently. If you really want to get what you think is due to you, now is the time to speak out. Rather than getting yourself involved in tasks that you can't see the other end of, it's worth concentrating today on things you can get out of the way quickly. Patience is not at its best now.

12 MONDAY   *Moon Age Day 23   Moon Sign Cancer*

There is now an emphasis on personal independence, so you may not take at all kindly to situations that seem to hem you in. What today is really about is is a greater sense of personal freedom, and woe betide anyone you wants to put extra responsibilities upon you. Even if money matters are variable, you can make definite progress with them.

13 TUESDAY   *Moon Age Day 24   Moon Sign Leo*

Getting things into perspective could now suddenly be much easier, assisting you to act as the voice of reason if arguments arise within your family or even at work. All the diplomatic skills for which Libra is justifiably famous can be put on display at the moment, and you shouldn't stick fast, no matter what the challenge might be.

14 WEDNESDAY   *Moon Age Day 25   Moon Sign Leo*

Is your ego over-inflated at the moment? You might think so, but this may not be the message you are getting from the world at large. Even if you've shown others that you can be more assertive, they shouldn't think any less of you for that. Extra demands in the professional sphere are ones you can relish and deal with very efficiently.

15 THURSDAY
Moon Age Day 26   Moon Sign Virgo

The pace of life may not be very fast just now because the Moon has now entered your solar twelfth house. This offers an opportunity to take more time to think, and perhaps to retreat into your own little world on occasions. If you can't find anything to worry about, younger family members could oblige you!

16 FRIDAY
Moon Age Day 27   Moon Sign Virgo

Be prepared to get a few details sorted out today because by tomorrow there may be less time to do so. The Moon is moving fast towards Libra, and offers a weekend that can be filled with potential excitement and new experiences. For now you should be on the ball in social situations, but may be slightly quieter in family and romantic settings.

17 SATURDAY
Moon Age Day 28   Moon Sign Libra

You have a magnetic personality at the best of times, but under present planetary trends you can ensure that almost nobody fails to recognise just how captivating you are. The weekend would be ideal for romance, and for finding exactly the right words to impress that very special person. Above all, today it is important to enjoy yourself.

18 SUNDAY
Moon Age Day 0   Moon Sign Libra

Self-confidence and a belief in your own abilities can now take you a long way. This is a very good time for new projects and for dealing with business and professional affairs. Of course this is a Sunday, so it is possible that the professional side of your life is on hold. If this is the case, don't be afraid to fulfil a few personal ambitions instead.

19 MONDAY
Moon Age Day 1   Moon Sign Scorpio

Sweet Venus is now in your solar first house, where it is more at home than in any other position. The focus is on romance in your life, and you can make the most of opportunities to sweep just about anyone off their feet. On a slightly negative side, any tendency to want to keep up with the Joneses today may well be a total waste of time and effort.

20 TUESDAY　　　*Moon Age Day 2　Moon Sign Scorpio*

A day to avoid acting on impulse, and to settle instead for what you already have. There is much to be said for making repairs rather than simply throwing things out and getting a new model, and this can be very satisfying as well. Above all, now is the time to avoid parting with cash unnecessarily, and to seek out value in everything you do.

21 WEDNESDAY　　*Moon Age Day 3　Moon Sign Sagittarius*

The emphasis is now on using your communication skills to get on well with co-workers and to put yourself in the good books of superiors. Away from work, today responds best if you are friendly, good to have around and filled with so much joy that you can please just about everyone. Any exceptions are probably best left well alone for now.

22 THURSDAY　　*Moon Age Day 4　Moon Sign Sagittarius*

Practical issues offer you scope for the best rewards, and you should continue to display a very capable but yet a distinctly successful impression. If you can get people to trust you, they should be pleased to involve you in their schemes. Financial progress is possible, but the emphasis today is on saving rather than spending.

23 FRIDAY　　　*Moon Age Day 5　Moon Sign Sagittarius*

You can now try to ensure that relationships and your love life are more harmonious than they have been for a while. Even if nothing in particular has been going wrong, there is now a gold-edged feeling to affectionate encounters. Make the most of surprises later in the day, which may be related to the attitudes of family members.

24 SATURDAY　　*Moon Age Day 6　Moon Sign Capricorn*

It cannot be ignored that Mars now occupies your solar eleventh house and this brings a slight change of emphasis. Don't be surprised if you end up rubbing others up the wrong way or getting on the nerves of someone you could do with cultivating. Your best response is to take a low profile when possible, and avoid talking too much.

25 SUNDAY   *Moon Age Day 7   Moon Sign Capricorn*

Libra is always eager to enjoy the sensual pleasures of life, but rarely more so than seems to be the case at the moment. Trends also encourage a strong interest in matters relating to your own security. You can make best use of this interlude by protecting your home more and maybe finding a different way to guard your valuables.

26 MONDAY   *Moon Age Day 8   Moon Sign Aquarius*

With your ruling planet, Venus, in such a strong position, single Librans especially can capitalise on an influence that supports fresh starts in the romantic sphere of life. Even those of you who have been committed to one attachment for many years can use it to discover ways to pep things up and to bring new romance flooding in.

27 TUESDAY   *Moon Age Day 9   Moon Sign Aquarius*

There probably won't be a more socially motivated time for you this month than you can experience around now. That's saying something, because Libra is probably the most socially inclined zodiac sign of them all. The focus is on seeking out good company and on doing all you can to make other people feel welcome and happy.

28 WEDNESDAY   *Moon Age Day 10   Moon Sign Aquarius*

It's time to get busy at work, though you also need to find ways in which you can mix business with pleasure. Even if making progress is quite easy, there are probably always one or two people who will use any excuse to avoid doing any work. You can afford to ignore such individuals and carry on in your own sweet way. Success is there for the taking.

29 THURSDAY   *Moon Age Day 11   Moon Sign Pisces*

You may well be inclined to seek physical pleasures at the moment, mainly because the Sun has now moved into your solar second house. This is a good time to build up personal securities and a period that demands great concentration on your part. Stay away from things that are purely theoretical in favour of sure-fire certainties of any sort.

30 FRIDAY
Moon Age Day 12   Moon Sign Pisces

A high degree of give and take is possible at this time, and is a legacy of that first-house Venus. Make sure you show your vivacity and warmth to everyone you meet, and it's also worth paying special attention to your appearance, both today and across the weekend. Once again you can allow the light of love to shine in your eyes – big time!

31 SATURDAY
Moon Age Day 13   Moon Sign Aries

If you want to make a good impression, you know you should be out there pitching. The problem is the lunar low, which has the potential to take the wind out of your sails. It just depends how much you want something, because the power to overcome obstacles is present. The simple rule of thumb is to persevere but not to exhaust yourself.

November

2009

1 SUNDAY
Moon Age Day 14   Moon Sign Aries

Obligations could prove to be a real test of your patience today. Energy is not at its highest, and there may be little you can do to improve the situation until tomorrow. Why not take a little rest and spend some time in company you find comfortable and mentally stimulating? It's probably better than doing anything dirty or unsavoury today.

2 MONDAY
Moon Age Day 15   Moon Sign Aries

If you've got your love life in good shape, you can now enjoy the accolades and affection that you have scope to attract at present. You might even be able to capitalise on some serious flattery, and this should please you no end. At work you would be wise to concentrate on those jobs you know are going to have the best results.

3 TUESDAY
Moon Age Day 16   Moon Sign Taurus

Trends allow you to be quite comfortable with repetitive work today and perhaps to take on those tasks that others find tedious or boring. Not that this means you have to be quiet or withdrawn. On the contrary, the livelier side of your nature can be put on display, and you can ensure that your approach to life is a joy as far as others are concerned.

4 WEDNESDAY
Moon Age Day 17   Moon Sign Taurus

Be careful about forcing your ideas and opinions onto others. Even if you are usually inclined to keep adverse or contentious opinions to yourself, this may not be the case under present influences. Family arguments are a distinct possibility, and these are probably best avoided if you don't want to get on the wrong side of anyone.

5 THURSDAY
Moon Age Day 18   Moon Sign Gemini

A day when there may be little point in arguing the toss about anything. It could be difficult to change anyone's opinion, and your own feelings are set in stone for the moment. Your best approach is to mix with people you find cheerful and diverting, and do what you can to avoid anyone who seems to be down in the dumps or grumpy.

6 FRIDAY
Moon Age Day 19   Moon Sign Gemini

What you encounter professionally today can help you to realise how much significant information you presently have at your disposal. Use what you know wisely and engineer situations to suit your own needs. It might seem as if you are being selfish, but actually this isn't the case if you make sure your actions benefit everyone.

7 SATURDAY
Moon Age Day 20   Moon Sign Cancer

You are now in a position to be disciplined and hard-working – maybe even slightly too much for your own good. Ask yourself whether some issues today could easily be left to sort themselves out, whilst you enjoy the strong social trends that presently surround you. It's worth planning well ahead when it comes to potential travel or changes at home.

8 SUNDAY
Moon Age Day 21   Moon Sign Cancer

You would be very wise to show a little care when it comes to pursuing luxury of any sort today. This is not because you don't deserve it, but simply on the grounds that you may not be getting the best value for money. A light touch works best when you are amongst friends, and can help you to ensure that your popularity is going right off the scale.

9 MONDAY
Moon Age Day 22   Moon Sign Leo

The focus now is on communication and on your need to get your message across in the way you intend. This shouldn't be at all hard for the average Libran, and now you can make use of the added advantage of Mars in your solar eleventh house. This is also a good time for climbing up the professional ladder, thanks entirely to your own initiative.

10 TUESDAY
Moon Age Day 23   Moon Sign Leo

Though positive for all practical affairs, the present position of the Sun does support a focus on one major task for today. If you can get yourself into the right frame of mind, your ability to stick at things could be little short of incredible. All that is necessary is a good dose of personal interest. A day to avoid boring jobs and boring people.

11 WEDNESDAY
Moon Age Day 24   Moon Sign Virgo

Your strength lies in your eagerness to help others in virtually any way you can. Some people might not be making this job any easier for you if they are refusing to do what is necessary to help themselves. Nevertheless, if you persevere you have a chance to win through in the end. You have what it takes to gain friends and influence people today.

12 THURSDAY
Moon Age Day 25   Moon Sign Virgo

The spotlight is on the finer things in life, and since this includes a little luxury, be prepared to make the most of whatever is on offer. There are times when all Librans need to sit back and relax, whilst someone else mixes the drinks and offers any necessary material support. You would be wise to avoid vexatious or insensitive people today.

13 FRIDAY
Moon Age Day 26   Moon Sign Libra

The start of the lunar high this month coincides with Friday the thirteenth. This fact will either be lost on you altogether or will be a source of amusement as you push on regardless. You can ensure that every sphere of your life prospers from the lunar high, particularly if you remain very positive and take advantage of extra good luck.

14 SATURDAY
Moon Age Day 27   Moon Sign Libra

The greater the challenge, the better you should now feel about taking it on. In fact it could be suggested that challenges are your greatest motivation at the moment. People you care about the most, either romantically or socially, are the ones you should be spending time with, and it may be necessary to spread yourself quite thinly at the moment.

15 SUNDAY   *Moon Age Day 28   Moon Sign Scorpio*

Money prospects have potential to improve, even if you don't exactly notice the fact in a moment-by-moment sense. Today offers you the odd new challenge of a social sort and should be quite stimulating in terms of your social contacts. Rather than sticking around the house too much right now, why not get out and about if you can?

16 MONDAY   *Moon Age Day 29   Moon Sign Scorpio*

You have what it takes to be especially good company for others under present planetary trends, and can easily mix business with pleasure to your own and your colleagues' advantage. The time is right to show how bright and intelligent you can be, and although this needn't be something you dwell on, it's helpful for boosting your popularity.

17 TUESDAY   *Moon Age Day 0   Moon Sign Scorpio*

In everyday matters there are serious considerations to be taken on board. Even if it is short-term plans that interest you the most today, you may also decide to look well ahead when it comes to intended journeys or full-blown adventures. Be careful with money because what look like cast-iron certainties now may not do so in a few weeks.

18 WEDNESDAY   *Moon Age Day 1   Moon Sign Sagittarius*

Trends encourage you to come up with ideas for greater financial independence and security – which is fine just as long as you are thinking about them but not doing anything concrete for the moment. It's worth taking time to consider all the implications. Meanwhile you have scope to get your love life working out just fine right now.

19 THURSDAY   *Moon Age Day 2   Moon Sign Sagittarius*

This has potential to be a relatively successful period, and although in some respects you have your work cut out, you have the ability to get through necessary tasks quickly and efficiently. What might be missing is a little excitement, and you will probably have to put this in place for yourself. Why not start thinking about plans for Christmas?

20 FRIDAY
Moon Age Day 3   Moon Sign Capricorn

Current planetary influences now favour all kinds of meetings or associations with people who are in a position to help you move forward in life generally. You can persuade almost everyone you meet to put themselves out on your behalf, and if you use your charms to the full, even strangers may be lining up to offer their timely encouragement.

21 SATURDAY
Moon Age Day 4   Moon Sign Capricorn

You may now decide that it's time for you to withdraw from things and to seek a little solitude. This probably isn't because you are out of sorts or tired of the world and all it offers. On the contrary, choosing to spend some time alone gives you an excellent opportunity to think things through – something you can't do in social situations.

22 SUNDAY
Moon Age Day 5   Moon Sign Capricorn

Being a natural fun-loving person, any tendency to isolate yourself is likely to be short in duration and now, once again, you can get yourself out there amidst the hustle and bustle of the world at large. Much of your energy can now be focused on creative projects and on sporting activities of one sort or another. A day to keep up with local news.

23 MONDAY
Moon Age Day 6   Moon Sign Aquarius

You have many mental gifts and a very active mind. You have a chance to use these under present planetary trends, and could well decide to turn your mind in the direction of something that stimulates your thought processes. You need to feel wanted too, and can take action right now that also helps to improve your popularity.

24 TUESDAY
Moon Age Day 7   Moon Sign Aquarius

Your love of diversity is only a disadvantage if you start too many projects at the same time. Even if you want to keep active, there is a limit, even for Libra, and if you take on too much you could become tired or flustered. There are good reasons to stay away from vexatious people and to stick to those individuals who are stimulating and good company.

61

25 WEDNESDAY   *Moon Age Day 8   Moon Sign Pisces*

Prepare to make sure that any practical tasks you have undertaken recently now begin to pay off. Small jobs should be no problem, and if you need to achieve anything major, relying on the good offices of friends and colleagues would be no bad thing. Take advantage of a strongly romantic interlude and the chance to make the very best impression.

26 THURSDAY   *Moon Age Day 9   Moon Sign Pisces*

Trends assist you to express your ideas at the moment and also to impress those individuals who have it within their power to elevate you in some way. Today is favourable for all intellectual pursuits and for coming to terms with necessary alterations that relate in some way to your home life or family interests.

27 FRIDAY   *Moon Age Day 10   Moon Sign Pisces*

Today has potential to start out quite well and extremely cheerfully on your part. What you may have to do is to come to terms with a few minor disappointments as the hours pass. This is because of the approach of the lunar low. By the evening you may decide to put your feet up, such is the effect of this influence on your energy levels.

28 SATURDAY   *Moon Age Day 11   Moon Sign Aries*

The signs are that this could be a slightly out-of-sorts today, especially when it comes to getting on with others. Although this is a very temporary state of affairs, it probably won't please you very much, particularly if you are keen to get on well with everyone. Show as much patience to your own nature as you do with that of everyone else.

29 SUNDAY   *Moon Age Day 12   Moon Sign Aries*

Any confusion at the start of the day can be made to disappear like the morning mist as the hours pass. If you use at least part of today for simple enjoyment you are more likely to end the day happy than you would if you take on jobs that require your full attention. By tomorrow you can make sure that the lunar low is nothing more than a memory.

30 MONDAY

Moon Age Day 13   Moon Sign Taurus

Trends stimulate your natural curiosity about everything at the start of this week, and with December just around the corner you also have a chance to think hard about the festive season and what you will have to do this year to make it special for everyone. If you use your organisational skills to the full, sorting things out should be fun.

December
2009

1 TUESDAY
Moon Age Day 14   Moon Sign Taurus

Mars remains in your solar eleventh house and this can, on occasions, be an argumentative influence. Instead of simply agreeing with others – or at least pretending that you do – you may now be more willing to cross swords with them. It probably won't do any harm to speak your mind. It's a chance to show others your opinions.

2 WEDNESDAY
Moon Age Day 15   Moon Sign Gemini

This is an ideal time to pursue travel or intellectual goals. Today responds best if you stay on the move, rather than allowing yourself to become either isolated or restricted in your movements. Prepare to welcome people you don't see too often back into your life, and to make the most of any opportunities for celebrity encounters!

3 THURSDAY
Moon Age Day 16   Moon Sign Gemini

Right now the focus is on talking, and on discussing ideas with just about anyone. Even people in the queue for the bus could seem interesting, as may those you meet in a casual way at work. Your home life might be less important for the moment, though younger family members could easily bring you back down to earth with a bump.

4 FRIDAY
Moon Age Day 17   Moon Sign Cancer

Professional developments are highlighted now, and there might be things happening in this sphere of your life that will cause you to think again about some of your strategies so far. Beware of getting tied down with boring or tedious routines, because these can prove to be extremely vexatious to the average Libran spirit.

5 SATURDAY · Moon Age Day 18 · Moon Sign Cancer

A slight element of indecisiveness is possible at the start of this weekend, though it is unlikely to stay around for very long. If there are only two possibilities in any given situation, you may well opt for tossing a coin, and in any case you might be so busy with social matters that there simply isn't time to jump about from foot to foot.

6 SUNDAY · Moon Age Day 19 · Moon Sign Leo

You can now benefit from a boost from other people, particularly if they think so much about you that they are putting themselves out on your behalf. Be prepared to get into the swing of social events this weekend and do what you can to cheer up anyone who seems to be having problems. You can ensure your love life is settled under present trends.

7 MONDAY · Moon Age Day 20 · Moon Sign Leo

You have what it takes to handle several different tasks at the same time today, and with the Sun now in your solar third house one of the most important factors in your life will be communication with others. Concern for the underdog is strong and you can afford to be in a very charitable frame of mind throughout most of this week.

8 TUESDAY · Moon Age Day 21 · Moon Sign Virgo

Mentally speaking this may not be the clearest day of the week. This is because of the position of the Moon in your chart and is, fortunately, a very temporary factor. There may be a slight tendency for you to retreat into your own shell, and you could well be happier with your own company than would normally be the case for Libra.

9 WEDNESDAY · Moon Age Day 22 · Moon Sign Virgo

Even if getting along with others is normally easy for you, trends suggest you may have difficulties with certain individuals at the moment. In particular, you probably won't enjoy being told what to do, even on those occasions when you know the advice is genuinely for your own good. Try to be philosophical about things for now.

10 THURSDAY
Moon Age Day 23   Moon Sign Libra

The Moon moves into Libra, and suddenly everything starts to look very different indeed. You can be right on the ball when it comes to getting what you most need from life, and should be able to get Lady Luck on your side. A day to get into the swing of social activities and let it be known that Mr or Miss Libra is up for a good time!

11 FRIDAY
Moon Age Day 24   Moon Sign Libra

You now have scope to show the pioneering side of your nature. If anything needs testing out, no matter what the inconvenience might be, you have what it takes to put yourself in the frame. Of course, taking real risks wouldn't be sensible, but a bit of adventure would be no bad thing. Make sure pre-Christmas events go with a real zing.

12 SATURDAY
Moon Age Day 25   Moon Sign Libra

Things should still be looking good, and the weekend will offer you more scope for excitement and a greater chance for you to show your social side. You shouldn't have to look very far for popularity, because most of the time it will be staring you in the face. Find the right words to whisper into the ear of that very special person this weekend.

13 SUNDAY
Moon Age Day 26   Moon Sign Scorpio

Co-operating with others is part of what today is about, and when it comes to having a good time you may well be happy to fall in line with the group. If doing things on your own doesn't appeal at all for the moment, there is much to be said for seeking out the company of friends. Make the most of chances to bring new personalities into your life.

14 MONDAY
Moon Age Day 27   Moon Sign Scorpio

As a slight contrast to yesterday, trends encourage a more independently minded Libra today. This might be particularly relevant in a work sense, and you need to realise that some of your colleagues could find you remote and unwilling to compromise. If you know the result you want, you may feel it is easier to achieve it on your own.

15 TUESDAY   *Moon Age Day 28   Moon Sign Sagittarius*

New information and ideas you are able to glean at this time can help you to enhance your life and to increase your confidence about your actions henceforth. Being an Air-sign individual, you may not have quite got your head round the fact that Christmas is imminent. Why not do that Christmas shopping just as soon as you have a few minutes?

16 WEDNESDAY   *Moon Age Day 0   Moon Sign Sagittarius*

What really turns you on as far as others are concerned is their intellect. That is why it's worth actively seeking out individuals who are bright and who have fascinating information to impart. You could so easily be disillusioned if you find yourself surrounded by people you think of as being loutish, boring and rude.

17 THURSDAY   *Moon Age Day 1   Moon Sign Capricorn*

You need the security of the familiar today, and this is one of the days of December during which there are good reasons to look very closely at your home surroundings. Maybe the time has come to have a heart-to-heart with your partner or someone to whom you are very close. Today is also ideal for clearing the air over disputes, perhaps at work.

18 FRIDAY   *Moon Age Day 2   Moon Sign Capricorn*

Once again it is communication that is emphasised the most. If someone close to you has had a very good idea, there is much to be said for discussing it at length with them. You can easily get yourself onto the same wavelength as others and can use today to get to know new individuals whenever circumstances allow you to do so.

19 SATURDAY   *Moon Age Day 3   Moon Sign Capricorn*

The focus is on your sharp mind and your powers of discrimination. Anything you take on today in the way of a contract or a new commitment can be worked out to your advantage, particularly if you make sure you know all the details first. If others forget things at the moment, perhaps you should come forward and remind them.

20 SUNDAY
Moon Age Day 4   Moon Sign Aquarius

The emphasis on pleasure is quite intense at this stage, and you can afford to have a good time in the company of people you both love and respect. What would be less beneficial would be to mix with people you see as being idiots or individuals who are loud or common. It's typical of Libra to mix only with those who are stimulating.

21 MONDAY
Moon Age Day 5   Moon Sign Aquarius

Have you forgotten again that Christmas is just around the corner? It's a distinct possibility, especially if you are busy doing other things. Now is the time to make yourself get out those boxes of decorations and to address the Santa Claus lists before it's too late. There's nothing wrong with a shopping spree right now.

22 TUESDAY
Moon Age Day 6   Moon Sign Pisces

Get ready to make this a very enjoyable phase in all domestic matters and to seek out the company of family members once the cares of the day are dealt with. Even if you don't feel much like working hard at the moment, you do have the resources necessary to get others to do things on your behalf and to be happy about the fact.

23 WEDNESDAY
Moon Age Day 7   Moon Sign Pisces

Getting everything sorted out to your satisfaction at work should offer you scope to do whatever takes your fancy once jobs are out of the way. There are strong social incentives around now, and you can make best use of these by surrounding yourself with friends. Beware of being too quick to find fault with other people's arrangements.

24 THURSDAY
Moon Age Day 8   Moon Sign Pisces

Last-minute details can be sorted out today, and Christmas Eve could find you up for almost any sort of challenge that comes your way. Influences may be less positive on the health front, though you have what it takes to shrug off any problems quite quickly. A feeling of contentment can be achieved by the evening.

25 FRIDAY   *Moon Age Day 9   Moon Sign Aries*

It's a fact that Christmas Day for you this year coincides with the lunar low. As long as you are aware of this fact, you needn't let it get in the way of you having an enjoyable day. If you don't feel the urge to travel far, it's worth considering staying among those you love. A day to avoid tedious conversations with anyone.

26 SATURDAY   *Moon Age Day 10   Moon Sign Aries*

You still may not be feeling on absolutely top form, and might have to work harder than usual to raise the necessary enthusiasm for anything associated with Christmas that you don't particularly like at the best of times. Why not seek out something to tax your intellect and intelligence, or simply spend some time on your own?

27 SUNDAY   *Moon Age Day 11   Moon Sign Taurus*

Now you have scope to get back to normal, and should have plenty of zest for the sort of parties that didn't appeal to you for the last couple of days. Even if everyone else is winding down and simply wants to sit still and let the whole thing digest, you can make the most of today by pushing for more excitement and getting other people to take part.

28 MONDAY   *Moon Age Day 12   Moon Sign Taurus*

Due to your natural sensitivity you won't allow others to upset you – though heaven knows one or two of them may well try. Be prepared to remain diplomatic and ready to please, though there could be moments today when you might 'tell it as it is'. Avoid getting on the wrong side of people you know are going to be important to you.

29 TUESDAY   *Moon Age Day 13   Moon Sign Taurus*

This is a time for asserting yourself. If you are back at work the opportunities surrounding you could be so much greater, but even if you are not you can find ways to push the bounds of the possible. Any new or ingenious idea you might have should be pursued for all you are worth between now and the New Year.

30 WEDNESDAY *Moon Age Day 14* *Moon Sign Gemini*

The need to simply take off and explore the world is strongly highlighted around now. The present astrological trends stimulate your thinking processes and can take you to a new and more interesting level where certain matters are concerned. Concern for family members is also important, though maybe not quite as much as usual.

31 THURSDAY *Moon Age Day 15* *Moon Sign Gemini*

Family matters are key on the last day of the year, and a journey into the past certainly isn't out of the question. You may decide to end the year on a high note by taking care of party arrangements yourself. Now is the time to be aware of any strange situations developing amongst your friends, and to avoid being left out when it comes to juicy gossip.

LIBRA:
2010 DIARY PAGES

LIBRA:
2010 IN BRIEF

B e as optimistic as possible as the year begins and enjoy the cut and thrust of a very busy working and social life. January and February should bring you more of what you need, even if you don't always get exactly what you want. There are possible gains to be made with regard to love, and you should feel warm and secure despite the inclement weather. Don't get too tied down by unnecessary red tape.

As the early spring arrives you might be feeling more like testing yourself, and there should be plenty of opportunities to do so. March and April will bring better organisational skills and a feeling that your efforts are now more appreciated. In terms of your courage and stamina you should now be up for anything, and you shouldn't easily give in when you know that the path you are choosing is the right one.

May and June look like being very fortunate months. As the weather improves and the lighter nights are in evidence, you will be filling your days with new potentials and probably also spending much more time out of doors and amongst people you recognise as being adventurous and exciting. This is not a time for you to hide your light under a bushel and you need to let the world know you are around.

The high summer and July and August should bring you yet closer to some of your heart's desires. There are gains to be made in terms of your financial standing, and you may be in the market for a major alteration at work. Librans who have been thinking about a change of house are more likely to embark upon such an adventure at this time and you will also be more inclined to travel long distances. This is a time to contact people you haven't seen for ages.

Although you could be slightly quieter at the beginning of September this will be a very temporary state of affairs. Everything comes together at the end of September and during October to offer you one of the best periods of the year. Give yourself fully to new projects and accept the romantic benefits that both months offer. Family ties strengthen and romance has probably never looked so good.

The final months of the year, November and December, see you consolidating on some of your recent gains and you should also be in a far better position to influence people and situations. Your silver-tongued eloquence means you make a good impression on some fairly important people and you will have what it takes to move a few personal mountains. Christmas should prove to be quite memorable.

January 2010

1 FRIDAY ☿ *Moon Age Day 16 Moon Sign Cancer*

You have scope to make this a good and encouraging start to the year. The Sun is presently in your solar fourth house, supporting extra concern for family members, though whether this is strictly necessary remains to be seen. As far as the practical side of your nature is concerned, it's time to come up with important new ideas.

2 SATURDAY ☿ *Moon Age Day 17 Moon Sign Cancer*

Today is about knowing your own mind and not being easily swayed by argument, unless you think that what is being said has genuine merit. You can afford to remain quite cheerful, and this would be an ideal time to get on with things that have been difficult or impossible whilst the Christmas festivities were taking place.

3 SUNDAY ☿ *Moon Age Day 18 Moon Sign Leo*

There could be plenty to keep you occupied today, though this is hardly surprising for Libra, which doesn't know the meaning of the word 'boredom'! Make the most of positive feedback you can attract from others, and of any opportunities to make gains in terms of finances – maybe as a result of some speculation on your part.

4 MONDAY ☿ *Moon Age Day 19 Moon Sign Leo*

Ordinary responses may not work today and you will have to be quite original if you want people to remember you. That shouldn't be too difficult for you and you can continue to benefit from the present run of good luck that is available. Professional relationships could cause you some small anxiety around now.

5 TUESDAY ☿ *Moon Age Day 20   Moon Sign Virgo*

A quieter couple of days are now on offer. The Moon is in your solar twelfth house and that means you have a chance to think. You needn't feel obliged to push yourself forward when in company and can use this interlude to listen carefully to what is being said around you. For once you will not be rushing your fences.

6 WEDNESDAY ☿ *Moon Age Day 21   Moon Sign Virgo*

If you decide to look out at the world from your own little corner you can get to grips with any plans that have been complicated by your usual busy routine. Now you can focus on things more clearly, and this would be an excellent time to use your intuition to assess the possible behaviour of friends and colleagues alike.

7 THURSDAY ☿ *Moon Age Day 22   Moon Sign Libra*

Today the Moon moves into your own zodiac sign of Libra. This brings that part of the month known as the lunar high and marks a potentially successful and enterprising period for you. You can ensure that people want to have you around by contributing to whatever is taking place, and you can take advantage of more luck than is sometimes the case.

8 FRIDAY ☿ *Moon Age Day 23   Moon Sign Libra*

You have what it takes to be very creative in your thinking today and to persuade others to follow your lead, probably without thinking too much about the situation. Getting to grips with thorny problems should be within your abilities, and you can move speedily from one task to the next. An ideal day to mix business with pleasure.

9 SATURDAY ☿ *Moon Age Day 24   Moon Sign Scorpio*

Your natural ability to get on with just about anyone can definitely be used to your advantage around now. Anything that is attainable should be completed in record time and even things you previously thought impossible could be within your reach. Even if you benefit from someone else's bad luck, you needn't feel bad about the fact.

74

10 SUNDAY ☿ *Moon Age Day 25* *Moon Sign Scorpio*

Heavy workloads are possible, though you needn't let them hold you back because you have a tremendous capacity for getting things done. The spotlight is on home-based demands whilst the Sun is in your solar fourth house, and you may have to think things through in new ways in response to relatives and even your partner.

11 MONDAY ☿ *Moon Age Day 26* *Moon Sign Sagittarius*

Your energy levels are enhanced, allowing you to put yourself out for the sake of others at this time. Newer and better chances to get ahead in your career are there for the taking, even if it is difficult to recognise some of them at first. Libra could be quite romantically inclined this week, so be prepared to impress your lover.

12 TUESDAY ☿ *Moon Age Day 27* *Moon Sign Sagittarius*

Rules and regulations could well get on your nerves if you allow them to do so. Do what you have to today, but beware of getting tied up in red tape because that will only lead to frustration. It might be better to ring the changes as much as you can and to opt for interests outside of work that are fresh and new. Do friends need your support now?

13 WEDNESDAY ☿ *Moon Age Day 28* *Moon Sign Sagittarius*

Trends suggest you know what you like and you like what you see when it comes to your social life around this time. There are many different sorts of people around and you can get the very best from all of them. What's more, you shouldn't have to work hard in order to do so. If people like you instinctively, that can be a great advantage.

14 THURSDAY ☿ *Moon Age Day 29* *Moon Sign Capricorn*

If your emotions are a little up and down at the moment, this could be the influence of the present position of the Moon. It's all very well being able to achieve a good degree of success, though there could be something inside you that yearns for more. A little dissatisfaction is natural from time to time, and there's no need to overreact to it.

15 FRIDAY ☿ *Moon Age Day 0   Moon Sign Capricorn*

It could be plain sailing today in terms of love and romance, and you can make the most of the positive attention you attract. This would also be an ideal day for Librans who are not emotionally attached to make a connection with a very special person. Don't be too hopeful about making a lot of money for the next few days. Never mind, sufficient is enough!

16 SATURDAY ☿ *Moon Age Day 1   Moon Sign Aquarius*

The weekend has potential to offer new diversions and a wealth of interests to help you brighten your waking hours. Your strength lies in your optimistic view of life and your ability to make the most of almost any situation. Newer and better ways of attracting money are on the way, but are probably only at the thinking stage for the moment.

17 SUNDAY *Moon Age Day 2   Moon Sign Aquarius*

Make this a day for doing whatever takes your fancy and unless you positively have to work today, don't do so. If you decide to put certain domestic tasks on the shelf for a while, this should leave you the time you need to enjoy yourself alongside people you really like. A day to ensure there is much laughter about, mostly originating from you!

18 MONDAY *Moon Age Day 3   Moon Sign Aquarius*

It's time to realise that life is not a rehearsal and that you will have to put in masses of extra effort if you want your performance to draw the attention of the crowd. If you manage to get superiors to notice you at work, that gives you an extra chance to impress, which could lead to a stronger financial base for the future.

19 TUESDAY *Moon Age Day 4   Moon Sign Pisces*

What you feel like inside and the way you come across to the world at large can be two very different things under present trends. Even if you are shaking in your boots you can portray yourself as confident and calm. It should now be possible to move towards specific situations that have been blocked to you in the past.

20 WEDNESDAY   *Moon Age Day 5   Moon Sign Pisces*

Keep up the pressure, at least until tomorrow. You still have it within you to turn heads, in both your social and working life. An ideal time to focus on your career, particularly if you have been unemployed for a while. Pay attention because some opportunities could be available in places you would not normally expect.

21 THURSDAY   *Moon Age Day 6   Moon Sign Aries*

Now the Moon moves into your opposite zodiac sign of Aries and that brings the part of the month known as the lunar low. This supports a quieter interlude when you can afford to take a well-earned rest rather than pushing yourself forward. Don't expect Lady Luck to dog your footsteps until the latter part of the weekend.

22 FRIDAY   *Moon Age Day 7   Moon Sign Aries*

You should still be happy to look out at the world from inside your own shell, though a quiet approach could confuse and even puzzle people who expect you to be lively and enterprising all the time. Why not let subordinates or even family members do things on your behalf? You can always disguise this need on your part as delegation!

23 SATURDAY   *Moon Age Day 8   Moon Sign Aries*

Although today will start out with the same quiet influences as have prevailed during the last couple of days, in the main you have scope to make this particular Saturday interesting and quite eventful. By lunchtime you can be right back on target and punching with the best of them. Even your sporting instincts are highlighted by present trends.

24 SUNDAY   *Moon Age Day 9   Moon Sign Taurus*

There may be something slightly odd about your thought processes whilst the Sun occupies your solar fifth house. You can use this trait to find original and new ways of looking at situations that have confused you in the past and to get the attention of people who could be useful to you. Some successes may now come unbidden and surprise you.

25 MONDAY   *Moon Age Day 10   Moon Sign Taurus*

Be prepared to complete the last lap of a race that has occupied you for a while, and whatever you decide to do this week, it's worth finding some time to reassess situations in the light of present evidence. Don't be surprised if others don't behave as you have come to expect. You can always change your own nature somewhat to suit circumstances.

26 TUESDAY   *Moon Age Day 11   Moon Sign Gemini*

Your best response to people who are still behaving in unusual ways is to play the chameleon and change colour to suit prevailing times. Fortunately this should be a piece of cake for Airy Libra, and you have everything you need to enjoy the cut and thrust of a busy and rewarding period. Making new friends is well accented today.

27 WEDNESDAY   *Moon Age Day 12   Moon Sign Gemini*

Out of complications come surprises and the opportunity to prove how clever you really are. Don't walk away from challenges today because these are the forges within which much success is created. One thing you may not relish at the moment is arguments – but then it isn't in your nature to be argumentative.

28 THURSDAY   *Moon Age Day 13   Moon Sign Cancer*

Be prepared to deal with difficult behaviour from friends and relatives. You have what it takes to find ways to rise above such situations and to pour oil on troubled waters. There are more financial gains on offer for Librans who keep their wits about them, and your ability to attract some amazing compliments has never been better.

29 FRIDAY   *Moon Age Day 14   Moon Sign Cancer*

Once again the attitude of those around you could cause the odd difficulty, and it may seem as though life is an uphill struggle in some respects. There is much to be said for showing the world just how much you know, and for making sure you have a chance to socialise too. Don't get tied down with boring or pointless tasks.

30 SATURDAY
Moon Age Day 15   Moon Sign Leo

Newer and better possibilities are available, especially if you are able to mix with Fire-sign people. These are individuals born under Aries, Leo or Sagittarius, but it is the bright and sunny Leos that you are likely to get on with the best. Your own nature is very warm and you can use it to bring a little bit of summer to the dark days of winter.

31 SUNDAY
Moon Age Day 16   Moon Sign Leo

The way you express yourself is quite important on this particular Sunday. What you get now is directly proportional to the amount of effort you are willing to put in. By all means keep up with jobs that have been piling up at home. You can make them more enjoyable by enlisting the support of others, particularly those who are good company.

February
2010

1 MONDAY
Moon Age Day 17   Moon Sign Virgo

The need to retreat from the world into a quiet little space of your own is quite natural on the first day of February. This is influenced by the entry of the Moon into your solar twelfth house and is not a trend that will last very long. You may decide you are happy to settle for second-best for today and tomorrow, but that's fine for now.

2 TUESDAY
Moon Age Day 18   Moon Sign Virgo

There may be opportunities to improve your domestic situation, and today is about achieving as much as you can without moving any further from your home and family than proves to be necessary. Any social reluctance you feel at present is down to a trend that lasts only until the later part of today.

3 WEDNESDAY
Moon Age Day 19   Moon Sign Libra

A definite change of planetary emphasis now brings along a much more positive phase and you can use this to return to being the sort of go-getting individual you often are. Be prepared to act swiftly whilst the lunar high is around and don't wait to be invited to do anything that you know is going to improve your life.

4 THURSDAY
Moon Age Day 20   Moon Sign Libra

All matters are positively helped by the position of the Moon, and you should be more than able to assist others as you forge your own path in life today. Now is the time to make full use of your instincts, together with a good dose of common sense. The emphasis is on your energy levels and your willingness to take the odd risk.

5 FRIDAY
Moon Age Day 21   Moon Sign Scorpio

In a social sense you have scope to benefit from some positive trends. Your best approach is to fill your diary and be willing to mix with all sorts of individuals, some of whom may not get on too well with each other. The tolerant side of your nature is to the fore, which of course is one of the traits that help you to gain the respect of others.

6 SATURDAY
Moon Age Day 22   Moon Sign Scorpio

Now you can make the most of a potential winning streak, and you shouldn't be tardy when it comes to pushing your luck as far as you can. It is said that we make much of our own luck in life, and that's certainly the case for Libra. Ask yourself whether you need to think more carefully about the attitude of your lover or family members.

7 SUNDAY
Moon Age Day 23   Moon Sign Scorpio

There are signs that getting on well with others might be a slight problem for you in some cases. Even if you are no less caring or co-operative than usual, there may be some people who are never satisfied, no matter how much you put yourself out for them. Your best response is to shrug your shoulders and move on to people who do appreciate you.

8 MONDAY
Moon Age Day 24   Moon Sign Sagittarius

You learn something new every day and there is little doubt that your versatility is your best aid at this time. It's a question of turning your mind in new directions at the drop of a hat and refusing to continue doing things in the same old way, simply for the sake of convention. A light, bright attitude is the order of the day now.

9 TUESDAY
Moon Age Day 25   Moon Sign Sagittarius

Your love life could be the most rewarding area at the moment, particularly if you are willing to keep up a positive attitude and seek out romance whenever you can. For some Librans there are new love interests in the offing, though it's worth being careful not to allow jealousy to arise between your most ardent admirers.

81

10 WEDNESDAY   *Moon Age Day 26   Moon Sign Capricorn*

If domestic matters turn out to be rather tiresome, you may decide to concentrate instead on work and your social life. Younger family members especially could be the source of problems, and it might even seem as though everyone you are close to has a very definite attitude at the moment. A day to stay away from confrontation.

11 THURSDAY   *Moon Age Day 27   Moon Sign Capricorn*

Chance encounters could now encourage you to think again about something you thought you understood only too well. There is nothing wrong with deciding to change horses in midstream in any sphere of your life under present planetary trends. Fortunately you are born of a part of the zodiac that is as adaptable as could be.

12 FRIDAY   *Moon Age Day 28   Moon Sign Aquarius*

You can capitalise especially well on opportunities at work and shouldn't have any difficulty coming to terms with any rearrangements or changes that come like a bolt from the blue. Your flexible approach can assist you to do something very different when you are away from work, maybe in order to enliven your social life.

13 SATURDAY   *Moon Age Day 29   Moon Sign Aquarius*

Your ability to get along with others now assists you to hog the limelight a little more than would usually be the case. You normally share only too well, but you have a chance to do better for the moment if you are out there in the lead. Stand by to attract some really significant compliments, and to react to them with your usual modesty!

14 SUNDAY   *Moon Age Day 0   Moon Sign Aquarius*

Prepare to enjoy an even higher profile amongst your friends today and to do all you can on this particular Sunday to get out and about as much as possible. Don't stay behind closed doors, even if the weather is horrible. The more you mix with others, the greater are the number of opportunities that should be available to you.

15 MONDAY
Moon Age Day 1   Moon Sign Pisces

Routine life need not be a battle for you at the moment, though you may have to be even more adaptable than would normally be the case if you really want to make progress. If others are determined to interfere in your projects, it's up to you to point the fact out. As always, diplomacy works best and helps you to avoid making enemies.

16 TUESDAY
Moon Age Day 2   Moon Sign Pisces

Co-operative and teamwork matters could seem somewhat less rewarding as the planetary influences around you begin to change a little. Having to fit in with the wishes of others could well prove to be somewhat annoying on occasions. There is much to be said for rehearsing what you are going to say in any public situation.

17 WEDNESDAY
Moon Age Day 3   Moon Sign Aries

Your usual successful touch with others could now be more difficult to use, mainly thanks to the arrival of the lunar low. You may not have as much patience as would normally be the case, and being prepared to count to ten can really make the difference. It might be best to stick to your own devices whenever possible today.

18 THURSDAY
Moon Age Day 4   Moon Sign Aries

A day to take as few chances as proves to be possible and to avoid financial speculation when there is no guarantee of a significant reward. Trends suggest that your interests are best served today by spending time close to home, particularly if the outside seems somehow threatening.

19 FRIDAY
Moon Age Day 5   Moon Sign Aries

After a fairly sluggish couple of days you can start to build your energy and confidence and be ready for just about any challenge that life decides to throw in your direction. Finances may need a rethink, and it's also worth turning your attention towards family situations as the weekend approaches. Be prepared to support your friends.

20 SATURDAY   *Moon Age Day 6   Moon Sign Taurus*

This would be a really good time to get new ideas started, as well as a fine interlude for thinking through your intended strategies for the longer-term future. None of this needs to restrict you in any way. In fact, you can afford to be constantly on the move and more than happy to join in with social invitations coming your way.

21 SUNDAY   *Moon Age Day 7   Moon Sign Taurus*

The spotlight is on socialising as much as possible and on being willing to mix business with pleasure, especially if you are a weekend worker. Present trends assist you to use your keen insight to see your way ahead very clearly. Even if there are disagreements in the family, remember that you don't have to be involved in them.

22 MONDAY   *Moon Age Day 8   Moon Sign Gemini*

Expanding your mental horizons would be no bad thing and at the start of a new week there are all sorts of new possibilities beckoning you on. This is Libra at its best and you are in a position to exercise your right for independence, though without ruffling any feathers on the way. Your reactions now are instinctive and positive.

23 TUESDAY   *Moon Age Day 9   Moon Sign Gemini*

It's time to step up the pace of life, especially if you are a working Libran. It's all about remaining energetic and inspirational, even if you are occasionally faced with people who are about as negative as it is possible to be. Giving the right sort of advice to friends may be quite easy, but don't necessarily expect them to follow it!

24 WEDNESDAY   *Moon Age Day 10   Moon Sign Cancer*

Even if this turns out to be a day of demands and responsibilities, you needn't let these get in the way of you having fun. What happens in a professional sense today could be quite decisive and it might seem as though there is a great deal at stake. All the same you can afford to stay relaxed and to approach life in your usual cheerful way.

25 THURSDAY
Moon Age Day 11   Moon Sign Cancer

In terms of friendship there could be conflicts taking place, and it might be difficult to avoid being involved in one way or another. Your best response is to try to play the honest broker, and if possible to stand aside from a partisan approach, no matter how much people try to draw you in. Your neutrality should eventually prove to be a boon.

26 FRIDAY
Moon Age Day 12   Moon Sign Cancer

The sort of information that you can glean from others could prove to be invaluable in terms of your career and also with regard to your wider social life. This is no time to be reserved when it comes to getting involved in a little gossip, because you can learn so much as well as adding to the chatter. Don't allow people to underestimate you at this time.

27 SATURDAY
Moon Age Day 13   Moon Sign Leo

Co-operative discussions can be productive for all concerned, and you have what it takes to remain centre stage in terms of social possibilities and new happenings. Anything that has a bearing on the area where you live should be of interest to you, and your charitable instincts are especially well highlighted at this time.

28 SUNDAY
Moon Age Day 14   Moon Sign Leo

With the Moon entering your solar twelfth house, today could well have a rather topsy-turvy atmosphere. Do you feel as though you are being opposed by others on a regular basis? It would be best to avoid becoming involved in situations that can have no positive outcome as far as you are concerned.

March

2010

1 MONDAY
Moon Age Day 15   Moon Sign Virgo

Trends support a slight sense of discomfort in social situations today, so keeping your own counsel would be no bad thing if it proves to be possible to do so. It isn't necessarily that you are opposed to being in company. Rather, you could well feel happier working on your own. In quiet moments your mind can be more focused than ever.

2 TUESDAY
Moon Age Day 16   Moon Sign Virgo

It could feel as though you are waiting for something because there is a strong sense of anticipation about early in the day. This proves to be the case, because not long after lunch the Moon enters Libra and you can start to make full use of the energy you have available, and be more inclined to join in. A day to forget worries and bring back some optimism.

3 WEDNESDAY
Moon Age Day 17   Moon Sign Libra

You now have more scope to get Lady Luck on your side than across the last few days. Even if you aren't doing anything very different, under the lunar high you have what it takes to be in the right place at the best possible time to make gains. When it comes to your personal popularity, life could hardly be much better.

4 THURSDAY
Moon Age Day 18   Moon Sign Libra

This is an ideal time for leadership issues to be sorted out, and if you remain assertive at the moment it would be natural for people to turn to you for guidance. Whether you are likely to comfortable in this role beyond the next couple of days remains to be seen, but for the moment you can be the general, and the army wants to follow your lead.

5 FRIDAY   *Moon Age Day 19   Moon Sign Scorpio*

You have a remarkable talent for dealing with people at all sorts of
levels and can really show this under present trends. It doesn't
matter whether you are talking to people at the bus stop or
involving yourself in important business deals. What does matter
today is your ability to persuade others to listen to the voice of
reason you represent.

6 SATURDAY   *Moon Age Day 20   Moon Sign Scorpio*

Today is well marked for progress. The Sun is presently in your solar
sixth house, assisting your efforts in administrative tasks. There are
also good reasons for being on the move around this time, and it's
worth avoiding being tied down by either routine or commitment.
If people want to come along with you – no problem!

7 SUNDAY   *Moon Age Day 21   Moon Sign Sagittarius*

Further advantages are there for the taking now that Mercury is
close to the Sun in your solar sixth house. You have the ability to
use your personality in order to get on with other people and can
change hats in a flash. Be prepared to keep abreast of major news
and views at this time and join in with whatever is going on in your
local area.

8 MONDAY   *Moon Age Day 22   Moon Sign Sagittarius*

With the Moon in its present position you are encouraged to seek out
exciting new possibilities. Your communication skills are also well
marked, and it should be quite easy for you to express yourself in an
emotional sense. Get on with any jobs early in the day and save time
later for doing things that are not practical but can be very enjoyable.

9 TUESDAY   *Moon Age Day 23   Moon Sign Capricorn*

You now have the ability to get the optimum from your working life
and to show yourself in a very positive light when you are among
people. In most situations you have what it takes to be in the lead
and to convince people to defer to your opinions and wisdom.
There may be a few small niggles today relating to finances.

10 WEDNESDAY   *Moon Age Day 24   Moon Sign Capricorn*

There is now a focus on the strong views you hold on a whole range of matters, and on how forcefully you express them. This is so unusual for you that those on the receiving end are certain to take notice. Don't let discussions, which can be positive, turn to arguments, which are not. It's important to keep abreast of what is going on at home.

11 THURSDAY   *Moon Age Day 25   Moon Sign Capricorn*

Now is the time to bring some excitement into your love life and to make sure you show other people the general power of your personality. The only slight fly in the ointment is that it could be difficult to display your usual sense of humour, so you may not be quite so inclined to laugh at your own folly as you usually are.

12 FRIDAY   *Moon Age Day 26   Moon Sign Aquarius*

With the Sun now in your solar sixth house you are constantly encouraged to work on behalf of others and especially those you see as being less well off in one way or another than you are. The emphasis is on thinking ecologically at this time, so it's worth dreaming up new ways to recycle more and to save energy.

13 SATURDAY   *Moon Age Day 27   Moon Sign Aquarius*

A rather tense day is possible in terms of relationships, though this need not be a bad thing if you monitor situations carefully. Even if you are slightly on edge at the moment, that can help you to be more reactive and better placed to make instant gains. Beware of getting tied down with petty worries about things that are not important.

14 SUNDAY   *Moon Age Day 28   Moon Sign Pisces*

This is an excellent time for separating the worthwhile from the worthless, a talent that you can extend to most spheres of your life at present. It's a question of getting organised and working out exactly what you are going to need in order to fulfil your personal objectives for the future. Absent-mindedness shouldn't be a problem now.

15 MONDAY
Moon Age Day 0   Moon Sign Pisces

Work opportunities that come along around now can help you to achieve advancement. Some Librans might even be thinking about a change of career, or at the very least a move within it. Are you looking for a situation that leaves more time for other things? With some careful thought this could be possible.

16 TUESDAY
Moon Age Day 1   Moon Sign Pisces

This may seem like a standard sort of day with little to set it apart or to mark it as special. If this is the case you are not looking closely enough at the opportunities that actually surround you. Neither are you taking advantage of the very real assistance that you could gain from others, particularly those who have reason to be grateful to you.

17 WEDNESDAY
Moon Age Day 2   Moon Sign Aries

Avoid making any concrete decisions today or tomorrow, or at least if you do, make certain that you understand the implications of what you are taking on. If there are any small flaws in your thinking at present, the lunar low is likely to expose them and extra care is necessary when you are dealing with fragile relationships and family ties.

18 THURSDAY
Moon Age Day 3   Moon Sign Aries

Obstacles are possible and progress is limited – which is why it would be sensible to avoid doing more than you have to for today. Why not let others take the strain while you sit back and have a well-earned rest? Thinking time is essential for everyone, and is especially important to Air-sign individuals like Librans. Slow and steady works best today.

19 FRIDAY
Moon Age Day 4   Moon Sign Taurus

As a direct contrast to yesterday you should now be able to handle a number of different strategies at the same time. Being released from the restrictions of the lunar low can be like being shot from a cannon, and you may not have much time to please yourself today. All the same, there is great happiness to be gained from being busy at present.

20 SATURDAY   *Moon Age Day 5   Moon Sign Taurus*

There is a strong social boost available at present and it is brought about by Venus. This is your ruling planet and it can do you masses of favours whilst it sits in your solar seventh house. You can increase your popularity, especially amongst those you see as being important, and have everything you need to give a good account of yourself.

21 SUNDAY   *Moon Age Day 6   Moon Sign Taurus*

An instinctive sense of harmony pervades your life, assisting you to recognise what looks and feels just right. In discussions it's important to see both sides of all issues and your best approach is to be fair and unbiased if people require advice. This should be a strongly socially motivated sort of Sunday and one that offers fun.

22 MONDAY   *Moon Age Day 7   Moon Sign Gemini*

Prepare to make the most of lively interaction between yourself and colleagues. This is an ideal period for mixing with friends at every opportunity and for getting involved with anything new or exciting that is going on in your vicinity. Gains can come from multiple directions, and this is definitely a time for keeping your wits about you.

23 TUESDAY   *Moon Age Day 8   Moon Sign Gemini*

Professionally speaking you can take advantage of a peak and of a number of opportunities for success, many coming like a bolt from the blue. Actually there is nothing at all strange about what is going on, because if you stop to think about things you should realise that it is your wise past actions that are leading to the gains that are on offer now.

24 WEDNESDAY   *Moon Age Day 9   Moon Sign Cancer*

You get along well with others at the best of times, but this is especially emphasised under present planetary trends. You can turn even people who you would normally find difficult to deal with into pussycats, and you should know how to adapt your own nature to suit prevailing circumstances. Libra can be really on form and buzzing now.

25 THURSDAY
Moon Age Day 10   Moon Sign Cancer

The Moon now helps you to make a success of teamwork situations and gives you more clout when it comes to putting yourself forward as a leader. There could be occasions when you doubt your own abilities, but this shouldn't last long. Libra is far more capable that it sometimes thinks itself to be, and now is definitely a time to shine when in a crowd.

26 FRIDAY
Moon Age Day 11   Moon Sign Leo

You can now make any sort of partnership work out well, and you have what it takes to co-operate fully and to make new friends on the way. Even strangers can be persuaded to warm to your personality at this time, and you can use your close relationships to modify your personality in a positive way. Libra's concern for others is to the fore.

27 SATURDAY
Moon Age Day 12   Moon Sign Leo

Be prepared to identify people who are important to your life and success, possibly to a greater extent than you had previously though. There's nothing wrong with asking for timely assistance, even from the most unlikely individuals. You public speaking abilities are also favoured at present. All in all you have scope to be on top form around now.

28 SUNDAY
Moon Age Day 13   Moon Sign Virgo

You would be wise to seek out a little peace and quiet in order to function perfectly today and tomorrow. The Moon in your solar twelfth house may encourage you to retreat into yourself, but this is only a temporary situation and shouldn't last long. Nevertheless it can be a useful period that ensures your planning is sound.

29 MONDAY
Moon Age Day 14   Moon Sign Virgo

A quieter time is still indicated, though that shouldn't matter in the great scheme of things because there is another potentially hectic period just around the corner. Clearing up any jobs that have been left over from the past would be an ideal way to start this week, as you prepare yourself for another significant push towards your chosen objectives.

30 TUESDAY
Moon Age Day 15   Moon Sign Libra

The lunar high offers a mental peak and a period during which you only have to think about something in order for it to become a reality. Of course you will have to keep your sights and expectations reasonable, but you do have what it takes to move the odd mountain. The support you attract from others can make all the difference at present.

31 WEDNESDAY
Moon Age Day 16   Moon Sign Libra

Lady Luck follows you around, even if you don't hear her footfall at every turn. You can use this influence to get the things you undertake today to work out well for you in both the short and the long term. You can also afford to start new plans or make commitments right now. Positive support is available from all manner of directions during today.

April

2010

1 THURSDAY
Moon Age Day 17   Moon Sign Scorpio

On the first day of April, make sure Libra isn't any sort of fool. Although the lunar high is now passing away for the month, you have little Mercury in your solar seventh house. This encourages a chatty approach and helps you to get the most from even the most casual of conversations. The practical joker in you can be clearly displayed at this time.

2 FRIDAY
Moon Age Day 18   Moon Sign Scorpio

You now have the opportunity to make agreements that are based on shared ideals and mutual benefits. This makes co-operation with others a dream, and decisions you make today can have a positive bearing on what comes along months down the line. If you're expected to shine in a social setting, you shouldn't let anyone down.

3 SATURDAY
Moon Age Day 19   Moon Sign Sagittarius

Ideas are the order of the day, and there is much to be said for sharing your notions with interested parties, in a professional sense but also in family settings. Today is partly about having fun, and present planetary trends assist you to sparkle and shine like a bright star. Don't be surprised, then, if others want to have you as part of their circle.

4 SUNDAY
Moon Age Day 20   Moon Sign Sagittarius

It's one thing to be put in positions that make you the centre of attention, but you might actually decide to seek these out yourself. By all means rehearse what you have to say when you are in social settings, though there is much to be said for spontaneity. That is the gift of the Libran nature and is part of what makes you so entertaining to know.

93

5 MONDAY   *Moon Age Day 21   Moon Sign Sagittarius*

This is a time when new partnerships are favoured, and a feeling of optimism attends co-operation of all sorts this week. Socially speaking a freewheeling mood works best, and there is much to be said for travel under present trends. If there are any frustrations today, they should be small ones.

6 TUESDAY   *Moon Age Day 22   Moon Sign Capricorn*

Domestic family relationships have potential to be more rewarding today than more distance attachments, such as colleagues. That needn't prevent you enjoying time spent with really good friends to whom you feel particularly close at the moment. At work it's not worth getting hung up on details. It's the bigger picture that counts.

7 WEDNESDAY   *Moon Age Day 23   Moon Sign Capricorn*

Personal attachments can now be intensified as Venus makes its presence felt in your solar eighth house. Meanwhile you have scope to think up some subtle tactics to use at work, and this might involve using the influence you have over others there. Even those in authority could be turning to you for help and advice at any time now.

8 THURSDAY   *Moon Age Day 24   Moon Sign Aquarius*

The spotlight is on how you enjoy your leisure time now and on the satisfaction you can gain through your inspirational nature. Doing things in different ways is part of the way you are made and is especially significant under present trends. Beware of getting carried away on a tide of optimism today, because a little realism is also called for.

9 FRIDAY   *Moon Age Day 25   Moon Sign Aquarius*

A day to be out there and enjoying yourself wherever there is action and excitement. Of course there are always responsibilities, but maybe you can find ways to take a short holiday from some of these for a day or two. Personal attachments now have a great deal to offer, and could be feeling different for some specific reason.

10 SATURDAY   *Moon Age Day 26   Moon Sign Aquarius*

An easy-going and plain-sailing time can be achieved on the relationship front, and this is especially true for Libran people who enjoy a stable, long-term attachment. This would be an ideal day to think up new ways to change your home environment to better suit your needs, and this has potential to be a very family-led and quite enjoyable interlude.

11 SUNDAY   *Moon Age Day 27   Moon Sign Pisces*

Trials and tribulations could turn up unexpectedly today, possibly at work, and most areas of responsibility might seem to be harder going than of late. The secret is probably not to get too involved in matters that are not your direct responsibility. Leave people to their own devices and don't offer unsolicited advice for now.

12 MONDAY   *Moon Age Day 28   Moon Sign Pisces*

You can now afford to make significant compromises in order to keep your nearest and dearest happy. This is also true at work, where you can find ingenious ways to keep those around you committed and content. If things don't feel quite right later in the day, bear in mind that the lunar low arrives tomorrow.

13 TUESDAY   *Moon Age Day 29   Moon Sign Aries*

A little confusion and tiredness is now possible, and there is much to be said for taking a break at this stage of the week. As long as you don't overburden yourself there is no reason why you should allow the lunar low to have any real bearing on your life during April. What you do need is variety, at least in terms of the way you look at the future.

14 WEDNESDAY   *Moon Age Day 0   Moon Sign Aries*

The Moon in Aries supports a degree of disorganisation and absent-mindedness, though if you are prepared to deal with this it needn't be a major source of frustration. Does it seem that people are avoiding you? It's worth asking yourself whether you have put up a metaphorical 'Do Not Disturb' sign, without even realising that you have done so.

15 THURSDAY   *Moon Age Day 1   Moon Sign Taurus*

Favourable highlights are now likely to surround personal relationships, and with the lunar low out of the way you can forge ahead towards some of your chosen destinations. By all means get rid of anything that isn't good for you, though actually kicking a habit might be slightly harder than you expected at this time.

16 FRIDAY   *Moon Age Day 2   Moon Sign Taurus*

Ego clashes that take place around now could well create a sense of frustration. Your best approach is not to get involved in such situations, though if you feel you are right about something, arguing the point will probably be your natural response. Be prepared to smooth out any areas of friction by putting in responsible effort.

17 SATURDAY   *Moon Age Day 3   Moon Sign Taurus*

Mental inspiration can be gleaned from travel and from seeing old things in a new and quite revolutionary way. The time is right to open your mind to new stimulus and to mix and match in terms of new situations and people who are only now entering your life. The more variety you can achieve, the greater should be your satisfaction.

18 SUNDAY   ☿   *Moon Age Day 4   Moon Sign Gemini*

Your social life could now be especially rewarding, and if you make the most of the new opportunities that are on offer you should enjoy this particular Sunday a great deal. Staying locked away at home is really not the best way to gain from all the possibilities of the day. It's better to move around.

19 MONDAY   ☿   *Moon Age Day 5   Moon Sign Gemini*

Minor conflicts are now possible, particularly in terms of professional projects. Seeing eye-to-eye with everyone may be quite difficult whilst the Moon occupies its present position. However, when it comes to your romantic life you needn't allow anything to stand in the way of your happiness and contentment.

20 TUESDAY ☿ *Moon Age Day 6 Moon Sign Cancer*

Personality clashes can still take place when you are dealing with the practical side of life, and your best approach is to remain as flexible as possible when you are dealing with anyone who seems determined to be awkward. It won't help to lose your temper because that will only lead to further complications. Better by far to count to ten.

21 WEDNESDAY ☿ *Moon Age Day 7 Moon Sign Cancer*

Personal and intimate attachments now come under the planetary spotlight, thanks once again to that potent position of Venus. You have scope to benefit personally, and perhaps even financially, through the involvement of a relative, and there is much to be said for seeking ideas from those to whom you are attached in an emotional sense.

22 THURSDAY ☿ *Moon Age Day 8 Moon Sign Leo*

There are gains to be made from being part of a group, and you can draw inspiration from the ideas of colleagues of friends. The only slight problem occurs if your feelings of independence prevent you from respond positively to be being told anything. It's really just a matter of being as flexible as the planets allow right now.

23 FRIDAY ☿ *Moon Age Day 9 Moon Sign Leo*

Trends encourage a drive to make changes to your home surroundings around this period. The need for a spring-clean may be especially strong at home but can also have a bearing on your working surroundings and the way you view them. A day to keep things light and airy and to get some variety into your social life.

24 SATURDAY ☿ *Moon Age Day 10 Moon Sign Virgo*

The sensitive side of your nature is highlighted at the moment, and you may even decide to withdraw from situations you see as being confrontational or unpleasant. It's natural to want everything to be warm and cuddly, but is it really necessary to take your bat and go home if things don't work out that way? Avoid getting annoyed about little things you can't alter.

25 SUNDAY ☿ *Moon Age Day 11 · Moon Sign Virgo*

When it comes to friendships, beware of getting so wrapped up in your own ideas and opinions at this time that you alienate some of your pals. Today works best if you can stay as open as possible to the suggestions of others, which could lead you to some very interesting places. It isn't like Libra to be stubborn, but that side of your nature is emphasised now.

26 MONDAY ☿ *Moon Age Day 12 Moon Sign Libra*

Trends encourage you to make up your own mind about virtually anything. Making your own luck is also the order of the day, and it's all about knowing how to be in the right place at the best time to get ahead. The lunar high offers golden opportunities for success across the next couple of days, and it's simply a matter of jumping on board the train.

27 TUESDAY ☿ *Moon Age Day 13 Moon Sign Libra*

You can maximise the possibility of success if you are willing to get the wheels of progress turning ever faster. Being part of almost anything that is taking place around you is one way to stay in touch with possibilities, and at the same time you can use your popularity in a social sense to become part of everyone's immediate circle!

28 WEDNESDAY ☿ *Moon Age Day 14 Moon Sign Scorpio*

The Sun has now moved into your solar eighth house and brings with it a period that is excellent for self-improvement and for any changes that you feel are long overdue. Your insights are clear and you can afford to follow them wherever they lead. Remember that you don't have to take everyone with you, especially people who are pessimistic.

29 THURSDAY ☿ *Moon Age Day 15 Moon Sign Scorpio*

Trends assist you to use your bright, quick mind to appreciate things in a flash. Looking at the big picture of life should be quite easy under present influences, and with that eighth-house Sun you shouldn't be at all put off by the prospect of major changes taking place. On the contrary, you might even be the one that inspires them.

30 FRIDAY ☿ *Moon Age Day 16* *Moon Sign Scorpio*

Be a seeker of wisdom and when you find it, pass it on. You have what it takes to persuade others to listen to what you have to say, and they could well act on your advice if you put it across well. Even individuals who have frustrated your efforts in the past can now be encouraged to follow your lead, so be prepared to make it worth their while.

May

2010

1 SATURDAY ☿ Moon Age Day 17   Moon Sign Sagittarius

You could be at loggerheads in a particular relationship and you may face criticism as a result. Your best response is to rise above your emotions and look at situations as impartially as proves to be possible. This is a weekend that can offer many social opportunities when you can create some fun at drop of a hat.

2 SUNDAY ☿ Moon Age Day 18   Moon Sign Sagittarius

Today could be a chance to spend some quality time in the company of intimates – your partner, family members or maybe a very close friend. Domestic challenges are the order of the day, and it's also a time for inspiring others to have fun, whilst at the same time achieving something that is very important.

3 MONDAY ☿ Moon Age Day 19   Moon Sign Capricorn

This could be a very good time for pleasure trips and for having fun in the company of people who have a very similar outlook on life to your own. Even if you feel are adventurous enough to try almost anything at the moment, a little care would be no bad thing where your own physical safety is concerned.

4 TUESDAY ☿ Moon Age Day 20   Moon Sign Capricorn

There are signs that partnership matters could absorb a lot of your time and energy during today. These could be of a business sort or, even more likely, personal attachments. If people can't or won't see things your way, your best option is to try to make them understand. Your patience is legendary and could well be tested under present trends.

5 WEDNESDAY ☿ *Moon Age Day 21   Moon Sign Aquarius*

Romance and high spirits are highlighted, encouraging you to convey a mood to the world at large that has excellent potential to attract others. Look out for romantic interests, even if you have not been particularly motivated by them recently. People who love to have you around may go to extraordinary lengths to make sure you are.

6 THURSDAY ☿ *Moon Age Day 22   Moon Sign Aquarius*

Ups and downs are a distinct possibility in close partnerships, but that is just the way the planets are panning out for you at the moment. You could well find that one minute you are getting on famously and the next you get annoyed at something that someone does or says. There are gains to be made today, but these tend to be subtle and infrequent.

7 FRIDAY ☿ *Moon Age Day 23   Moon Sign Aquarius*

Mars is now in your solar eleventh house, and one way it might have a bearing on your life is to make it difficult to discover where the real action is taking place. The practical side of your nature is highlighted, assisting you to get more things organised than might sometimes be the case. Don't be surprised if others laugh.

8 SATURDAY ☿ *Moon Age Day 24   Moon Sign Pisces*

A time of clear insights is on offer and you can use this to get things to fall into place this weekend, at least in your mind. Turning your thoughts into real situations could be rather more difficult, but if you manage to attract some goodwill there are gains to be made. Today is especially favourable for social gatherings and for travelling around.

9 SUNDAY ☿ *Moon Age Day 25   Moon Sign Pisces*

There is much to be said for making practical changes to your home and your general surroundings. You needn't be held back by convention, and should be willing to let go of anything that is holding you back. Lightening the load can certainly work wonders. Bear in mind that emotionally sensitive material should be dealt with carefully.

10 MONDAY ☿ *Moon Age Day 26   Moon Sign Aries*

Things may not be going entirely your way at the start of this particular working week. It's somewhat unfortunate having the lunar low around on a Monday, but it shouldn't prevent you from prospering in small ways. Be prepared to respond if your forward progress is restricted or if people generally seem less than helpful.

11 TUESDAY ☿ *Moon Age Day 27   Moon Sign Aries*

Trends support an interlude during which you may lack the capacity to concentrate hard on any one subject. Why not allow others to take the strain for the moment? That needn't prevent you making any sort of progress, even if it seems in some situations that you are taking one step forward and two back. A day to rely on your sense of humour.

12 WEDNESDAY ☿ *Moon Age Day 28   Moon Sign Aries*

Despite a potentially slow start today, it won't be long before the lunar low is completely out of the way and you can get back to the sort of Libran you have been recently. The Sun is still in your solar eighth house, so the spotlight is definitely on personal matters. Alterations in store could be the order of the day at home.

13 THURSDAY *Moon Age Day 29   Moon Sign Taurus*

It shouldn't have escaped your attention that the nights are getting lighter and the weather warmer. This offers you scope to show that you are by nature a free spirit and that you love to be outdoors whenever possible. It's worth spend some time today in the garden or walking in a local park. Allow your confidence and optimism to grow like the flowers.

14 FRIDAY *Moon Age Day 0   Moon Sign Taurus*

Even if you are having to contend with certain unhelpful individuals at this time, it's still worth trying to persuade others to help you on your way. Newer and better opportunities are on offer, especially at work, though it might be difficult to get hold of the specific information that would help you today.

15 SATURDAY   *Moon Age Day 1   Moon Sign Gemini*

This ought to be a really good time for trying out anything new. Your ruling planet, Venus, stands in your solar ninth house, beckoning the Sun on and offering different and exciting incentives. The more open-minded you remain at the moment, the better you can get things to work out for you. Be definite about any changes you want to make.

16 SUNDAY   *Moon Age Day 2   Moon Sign Gemini*

Today is about continuing to seek change and variety, if only for its own sake. New stimulus may be required if you want to achieve total happiness, but there may be minor obstacles to overcome, especially at home. It ought to be possible to rely on the good offices of friends and to persuade your partner to offer support.

17 MONDAY   *Moon Age Day 3   Moon Sign Cancer*

This is a time to concentrate on essentials, so there are good reasons to leave all the 'froth' of life alone for the moment. Let people know you mean business and they are likely to work alongside you, but be in any way flippant and help is not so available. It's time to take yourself more seriously, which might be a bit of a struggle for carefree Libra.

18 TUESDAY   *Moon Age Day 4   Moon Sign Cancer*

Some tension could now be accumulating, possibly at home, though it could just as easily be in the workplace. Bursts of temper might be your natural reaction, though this would be most unlike you. The odd harsh word isn't the end of the world, and in any case you won't stay mad for long. Be as kind as you can to anyone who is having problems now.

19 WEDNESDAY   *Moon Age Day 5   Moon Sign Leo*

The present position of Venus helps you to blow away any cobwebs that are still surrounding you after the winter so that you can be fully alert to the promise of the coming summer. A day to do something fresh and exciting if possible. You needn't settle for second-best when it comes to your own efforts at work or later at home.

20 THURSDAY
Moon Age Day 6   Moon Sign Leo

By all means concentrate on what seems most important, but leave time aside for having fun. You can't expect to be achieving something concrete all the time, and in any case you can find inspiration in the most random situations. What matters the most is your ability to pay attention, which enables you to pick up on so many opportunities today.

21 FRIDAY
Moon Age Day 7   Moon Sign Virgo

Make sure you are not a doormat to all-comers today. You need to be slightly more assertive and to let the world know you won't be put upon. The Moon in your solar twelfth house supports a slightly more withdrawn interlude, and this may be the reason that you appear to be off your guard. It's time to show others that this isn't the case.

22 SATURDAY
Moon Age Day 8   Moon Sign Virgo

Understanding the importance of charm is absolutely essential to the Libran character. You can get what you want from life using your wonderful nature rather than by stamping on others as you pass along life's road. This helps you to avoid making enemies, and today is about how much help you can attract from others when things get critical.

23 SUNDAY
Moon Age Day 9   Moon Sign Virgo

Although you may feel at first today as though you can't gain the speed you would wish in even normal situations, this state of affairs shouldn't last long into the day. Energy is there for the taking by the afternoon and you have a chance to display your optimistic slant on life. This evening can be fun from a social point of view.

24 MONDAY
Moon Age Day 10   Moon Sign Libra

The lunar high assists you to make the most of personal gambles. If you have decided on a particular course of action, this is the day to push forward into uncharted but exciting territories. Don't be afraid to rely on your own gut feelings and allow your natural talents to emerge. Life may well be on your side, but you still need to put in the maximum effort.

25 TUESDAY   *Moon Age Day 11   Moon Sign Libra*

Your instincts for making money are highlighted as the lunar high continues, so you can afford to gamble just a little because you are not really taking chances at all. Getting what you want from life should be easier now, particularly if there are people around who simply adore you and who would be willing to give you some support.

26 WEDNESDAY   *Moon Age Day 12   Moon Sign Scorpio*

The Sun has now moved into your solar ninth house, suggesting that you won't be dissuaded from seeking personal freedom, even if this means having to reorganise your life in significant ways. The focus is firmly on your need for fresh fields and pastures new, so it's hard to see how redundant thinking can play any part now.

27 THURSDAY   *Moon Age Day 13   Moon Sign Scorpio*

Attending to a variety of interests now allows you to get the very most from your life. This has potential to be a very busy phase, which is all the more reason to become fully committed to everything that is exciting and inspirational. The creative side of your nature is also emphasised, assisting you to make positive changes to your living space.

28 FRIDAY   *Moon Age Day 14   Moon Sign Sagittarius*

Making things go your way in a professional sense counts for a great deal at the end of the working week. There is much to be said for getting certain matters straight and leaving things tidy for later. You can also seek opportunities to enjoy yourself in the company of the sort of people you find exciting to be around.

29 SATURDAY   *Moon Age Day 15   Moon Sign Sagittarius*

Suppressed tensions today will do nothing to help in friendship matters. Even if problems are not of your making, you may have to deal with some of the awkwardness, and as a result you might be more comfortable amongst family members. This is a short lunar trend and everything should seem different by tomorrow.

30 SUNDAY
Moon Age Day 16   Moon Sign Capricorn

You can afford to be quite open-minded at this time, and this allows you to take a very different view of what might turn out to be a vital matter. The more philosophical side of your nature can now be put to use, enabling you to think deeply about all sorts of matters. There are small financial gains to be made, some of which may surprise you.

31 MONDAY
Moon Age Day 17   Moon Sign Capricorn

If you can't impose your will on others, why not leave well enough alone? This is not a time to interfere too much in the affairs of the world at large, especially if there are things that are important in your own life. Some surprises are possible later in the day, and this is an ideal time for participating in any sort of social challenge.

June

2010

1 TUESDAY
Moon Age Day 18   Moon Sign Capricorn

Mercury in your solar eighth house can help you to improve important business relationships and make the most of incentives of a practical nature that are on offer. Wherever financial or emotional support is necessary, it's a question of seeking out new situations and people to rely on. A fun evening can start June with a bang!

2 WEDNESDAY
Moon Age Day 19   Moon Sign Aquarius

You have what it takes to get along with others famously, especially under present planetary trends. This is of use to you in a number of different ways. Not only should your popularity make your social life more interesting, it also assists you in reacting to the emotional responses of others, and makes this a period in which romance is well marked.

3 THURSDAY
Moon Age Day 20   Moon Sign Aquarius

Venus has now moved on into your solar tenth house. This is a planet that is worth tracking in your chart because it is so important to you. In this position it increases your ability to communicate effectively and also ensures that you can get others to listen. This is a positive 'across the board' trend that assists you to improve your life.

4 FRIDAY
Moon Age Day 21   Moon Sign Pisces

Today is an opportunity to deal with tasks that demand great concentration. Your self-discipline is highlighted, and you can make the most of it when dealing with matters you would normally leave alone. At the same time you should discover that experience is definitely the best teacher, which is why you can undertake repeated jobs so efficiently.

5 SATURDAY   *Moon Age Day 22   Moon Sign Pisces*

A greater need for independence and freedom is symptomatic of trends this weekend. You may decide you would rather not be tied down by routine or the demands of family members. Remember that if there are jobs that you aren't keen to undertake on their behalf, it probably won't do them any harm to fend for themselves on occasions.

6 SUNDAY   *Moon Age Day 23   Moon Sign Pisces*

Look towards a Sunday that can be livelier and more exciting thanks to the way you embark on new adventures. These don't have to be big undertakings, but it would help if you are trying out things you haven't involved yourself in before. Romance is favoured at the moment, assisting you to turn heads without even trying to do so.

7 MONDAY   *Moon Age Day 24   Moon Sign Aries*

This could be a time when circumstances will block some of your plans, or at the very least make them slightly more difficult to accomplish. The best way to handle the lunar low is to allow time to pass whilst you take a well-earned break. You needn't balk at the thought of a few necessary routines around now.

8 TUESDAY   *Moon Age Day 25   Moon Sign Aries*

If it is harder today to get your message across, you can at least plan ahead for how you will change things again tomorrow. Rather than being restless, why not settle yourself to something quiet that you enjoy doing? You can seek reassurance from loved ones if required, and can make the most of the chance to catch up with people around your home.

9 WEDNESDAY   *Moon Age Day 26   Moon Sign Taurus*

You could be slightly in the dark as far as short-term finances are concerned and if this is indeed the case, it's worth doing some delving in order to establish what is actually going on. There are some positive gains to be made in terms of romance, and you should be able to achieve another increase in your general popularity.

10 THURSDAY   *Moon Age Day 27   Moon Sign Taurus*

When it comes to professional matters the focus is on working hard and making significant ground. Your strength lies in your present ability to forge relationships with superiors, without alienating yourself from colleagues. Once work is over the simple instruction at this time is to have some fun.

11 FRIDAY   *Moon Age Day 28   Moon Sign Gemini*

An ideal day for taking a journey and seeing the outside world. Even if you only have an hour or two to spare you can go somewhere. At the same time there is an emphasis on culture, so an art gallery, a museum or somewhere equally stimulating might appeal to you. Try to share your interests while the Sun occupies its present position.

12 SATURDAY   *Moon Age Day 0   Moon Sign Gemini*

Personal freedom is important to you at the best of times, but right now it seems to be essential. You won't be at all happy if you sense you are being restricted in any way, and having your wings clipped is probably not something you would allow under present trends. However, there's nothing wrong with sharing your adventures with others.

13 SUNDAY   *Moon Age Day 1   Moon Sign Gemini*

Positive financial trends are starting to build, even though things might not seem very different right now. Your best approach is to look and plan ahead carefully, making sure you are doing the best you can with any money you presently have. Even very small amounts can be made to work for you in a positive way. Help can be sought from friends now.

14 MONDAY   *Moon Age Day 2   Moon Sign Cancer*

It's possible that some projects and goals may not be quite as well thought out as you had hoped at the beginning of this week, or else others are finding ways to scupper your plans. Bear in mind that this may not be deliberate, so instead of losing your temper it might be best to laugh. Starting again might enable you to make things even better.

15 TUESDAY   *Moon Age Day 3   Moon Sign Cancer*

The Sun remains in your solar ninth house and while it is there it may be difficult to function well in any closed environment. Travel is the order of the day, even if it is only a few miles from home, and it should help you to reap the benefits from new situations you encounter. Routine may seem to be something of a curse today.

16 WEDNESDAY   *Moon Age Day 4   Moon Sign Leo*

It is possible that you could now experience a few problems in relation to friends. This is not necessarily the best time of the month for co-operation or harmony within groups. Where you could win out at the moment is with regard to personal ties. Romance should be high on your agenda, and the influences look very positive indeed.

17 THURSDAY   *Moon Age Day 5   Moon Sign Leo*

You can best avoid tensions at home by keeping busy away from your usual domestic surroundings. This problem, if it occurs at all, is tied to your present need for freedom and diversity. If you feel you are being restricted by responsibility it's a natural response to react somewhat harshly, but finding ways to change things is a better option.

18 FRIDAY   *Moon Age Day 6   Moon Sign Virgo*

The Moon is now in your solar twelfth house, encouraging a more thoughtful interlude in which you can retreat from certain situations more than you normally would. This doesn't mean you can't get involved in anything, merely that you might benefit from a few hours in which to please yourself. Make sure the people who love you understand.

19 SATURDAY   *Moon Age Day 7   Moon Sign Virgo*

It's worth keeping abreast of news and views within your community, though you don't have to become too involved for the moment. You would be wise to stand aloof from local issues and from the desire of others to make changes. By tomorrow a more active and reactive Libra can show itself, but there is much to be said for being a closed book now.

20 SUNDAY   *Moon Age Day 8   Moon Sign Libra*

Now is the right time to move upward and outward. The lunar high coincides with the movement of the Sun into your solar tenth house. A number of potentially successful opportunities are there for the taking. If these are professional in nature you might have to wait until tomorrow, but in the meantime, get planning furiously!

21 MONDAY   *Moon Age Day 9   Moon Sign Libra*

Now you can definitely put yourself in the right place to make significant headway and at the same time remain both cheerful and very persuasive. There's no need to wait around for things to turn your way because, as the saying goes, 'fortune favours the bold'. If there is something you really want, now is surely the best time to ask for it.

22 TUESDAY   *Moon Age Day 10   Moon Sign Scorpio*

There is now a strong emphasis on money and the chance to make more of it in the three or four weeks that the Sun occupies your solar tenth house. There are gains to be made from your ingenious ideas, and this is a favourable period to put these to the test. This is no time for watching and waiting. You need action and you can really make things happen.

23 WEDNESDAY   *Moon Age Day 11   Moon Sign Scorpio*

The chance to make new decisions and clear choices is yours for the taking. Your practical skills are highlighted, assisting you to put many of your plans into action. With ingenuity on your side you have scope to think up ways of doing things that never occurred to you before, and on the way you can score some genuine successes.

24 THURSDAY   *Moon Age Day 12   Moon Sign Sagittarius*

You can't stand things to be constantly untidy, and even if your mind is sometimes like a muddled workbasket, you probably prefer to live in congenial and clean surroundings. Trends emphasise this at the moment and so today is ideal for going from one place to another, putting things away and making everything spick and span.

25 FRIDAY   *Moon Age Day 13   Moon Sign Sagittarius*

At work an efficient and congenial approach should enable you to make significant headway. Librans who have been out of work for a while could discover something to their advantage before very long, and this adds to a general sense of optimistic now. The fact that you are good company allows you to gather friends around you.

26 SATURDAY   *Moon Age Day 14   Moon Sign Sagittarius*

Social and group relationships take on a new meaning for you now, and staying indoors is not the best use of this weekend. On the contrary, it's time to make the very most of all that this part of summer has to offer, and the luckiest Librans might even have set this period apart as a time for taking an early holiday.

27 SUNDAY   *Moon Age Day 15   Moon Sign Capricorn*

Most planetary trends now encourage you to turn your mind in the direction of private emotional issues, which offers you a slightly more contemplative interlude in which to talk things through with your partner. If family members have been difficult to deal with recently, this would be a favourable time to establish better contact with them.

28 MONDAY   *Moon Age Day 16   Moon Sign Capricorn*

You are now entering a vital period during which you can reach new highs in your thinking and put plans that have been around for quite a while into action. By all means look months into the future, though there is still plenty of scope for acting now. Don't be afraid to let your mind range across a broad spectrum of interests at this time.

29 TUESDAY   *Moon Age Day 17   Moon Sign Aquarius*

Confidence remains the key, and even on those occasions when you don't feel to have very much, you have what it takes to convince others that you do. Persuading people that you know what you are doing is the best way to get colleagues and friends to follow your lead. There is much to be said for double-checking details, especially those relating to meetings.

30 WEDNESDAY   *Moon Age Day 18   Moon Sign Aquarius*

Generally speaking the planetary focus is now on social pleasures and your love life. Even if you are still be busy in a practical sense, your interests are best served by putting aside some time to explore relationships more fully and to catch up with anyone you've been neglecting of late. The genuine concern of Libra is now clearly on display.

July

2010

1 THURSDAY
Moon Age Day 19   Moon Sign Aquarius

Your imagination is strong and you can use it to find new practical ways to solve any problems that have been dogging you for a while. The first day of July awakens you to possibilities you have not explored, and there might even be a tinge of excitement about. An ideal day for contacting those who live at a distance.

2 FRIDAY
Moon Age Day 20   Moon Sign Pisces

Today is well accented for work-related matters and also, later in the day, for getting closer than ever to your partner. Libra is always romantically inclined to some extent, but you have what it takes to be the lover of the century now! Remember that any sort of pretence is best avoided when dealing with issues that work better in the light of absolute truth.

3 SATURDAY
Moon Age Day 21   Moon Sign Pisces

By all means get on with professional goals if you can, though of course this might not be possible unless you work at the weekend. It's worth keeping your planning head on and using it to get things moving in every sphere of your life. Do restrictions bore you? An adventurous and freewheeling response is called for now.

4 SUNDAY
Moon Age Day 22   Moon Sign Aries

Delays and obstacles are possible whilst the lunar low pays its monthly visit, but you do have the advantage of knowing that it shouldn't have much of a bearing on your ability to move around freely. Whether you actually want to be quite as go-getting as you have been remains to be seen, but the opportunity is still there.

5 MONDAY
Moon Age Day 23   Moon Sign Aries

You may have some trouble getting all you want out of today because you have the lunar low to contend with. Keep up your efforts all the same because you also have some strong supporting planets, and although you might have to put in extra effort you can still win through. Unforced errors are possible, so pay attention.

6 TUESDAY
Moon Age Day 24   Moon Sign Aries

Getting hung up on punctuality isn't the best way of dealing with any delays that occur today. As long as you get where you want to be, does it really matter too much if you have to reorganise your schedule or rely more on others? By the evening you should be able to get yourself back on course as far as your favoured plans are concerned.

7 WEDNESDAY
Moon Age Day 25   Moon Sign Taurus

This is an ideal day to get to the heart of any personal matters and to become involved in deep and meaningful conversations with those to whom you are particularly close. The attitudes of friends aren't always easy to understand, and a little probing may well be necessary if you are determined to discover what is really going on.

8 THURSDAY
Moon Age Day 26   Moon Sign Taurus

With the Sun in your solar tenth house this has potential to be a good time for handling bigger responsibilities. You have scope to achieve something you have been wishing for for a while, and there are possible gains to be made in terms of savings and general personal finances. You might decide to defer some appointments today.

9 FRIDAY
Moon Age Day 27   Moon Sign Gemini

A day to find some way to improve your education or to broaden your knowledge base in terms of practical skills. It doesn't matter how old you are, because Libra is constantly learning something and is usually happy to do so. Try not to be too available for family members, who may well be taking advantage of your good nature.

10 SATURDAY   *Moon Age Day 28   Moon Sign Gemini*

As is usually the case you could be very obliging today. This is a boon under most circumstances, though not if you are being taken for granted. Such a situation is as likely to happen in friendship circles as it is at home. Today is about encouraging people to take responsibility for their own lives and especially for their own actions.

11 SUNDAY   *Moon Age Day 29   Moon Sign Cancer*

The emphasis in your personal life shifts from the superficial to the very deep. Be prepared to respond if your partner, or a close family member, wants to take you into their confidence about something that might slightly surprise you. Whatever the revelation may be, it would be sensible to try and take it in your stride without too much reaction.

12 MONDAY   *Moon Age Day 0   Moon Sign Cancer*

An expanded sense of self-confidence at work is achievable now. It's time to find out what is expected of you make sure you are able to deliver the goods. All may not be sweetness and light as far as colleagues are concerned, and it's a question of how you decide to deal with the possibility of envy or jealousy in your vicinity today.

13 TUESDAY   *Moon Age Day 1   Moon Sign Leo*

You can make sure your social life is the most rewarding area for today and perhaps for the remainder of this week. Success can be gained from group matters and from being able to rely on the support of many different people. If you are involved in situations that do involve others, don't be afraid to put yourself forward as the natural leader.

14 WEDNESDAY   *Moon Age Day 2   Moon Sign Leo*

You are in a position to use your energy to help others in practical ways, even if you know you can't do everything you would wish. Support can be obtained for some of your more outrageous schemes and for plans that have been at the back of your mind for weeks or months. Mixing with the right people might be especially important when you are at work.

15 THURSDAY   *Moon Age Day 3   Moon Sign Virgo*

Trends support a period of susceptibility to the influence of specific people. That's fine, just as long as you ensure that these individuals are reliable and that they are not somehow pulling the wool over your eyes. Going for any sort of extreme is not to be recommended right now, and a slow and steady pace works best.

16 FRIDAY   *Moon Age Day 4   Moon Sign Virgo*

Your strength now lies in your increased intuition and the sense you have of your own spirituality. This is enhanced by the position of your ruling planet, Venus, which presently occupies your solar twelfth house. With this trend also comes a strong awareness of what is exactly the right time to take specific actions. Listen to your inner voice.

17 SATURDAY   *Moon Age Day 5   Moon Sign Libra*

Your outlook remains enterprising, and you can afford to be just about as cheerful as Libra gets. This helps you to shine in company, and is a favourable sign for the weekend. The lunar high increases your chances of getting what you want materially and with Venus in its present position you can extend this to your romantic life too.

18 SUNDAY   *Moon Age Day 6   Moon Sign Libra*

Keep your self-confidence going from strength to strength. There are gains to be made from putting yourself in the best possible position to take up opportunities and you should be happy to try as many new possibilities as you can. By all means seek help from friends, and reap the benefits of your positive attitude towards them.

19 MONDAY   *Moon Age Day 7   Moon Sign Scorpio*

A slightly more cautious approach is encouraged today, and this is especially the case in terms of finances. It's worth taking a close look at your budget before you spend lavishly (or perhaps before you spend anything). On the personal front, you have a chance to make significant ground when it comes to impressing someone you care for.

20 TUESDAY
Moon Age Day 8   Moon Sign Scorpio

With reflection and detachment you can get a great deal of what you want from life, though probably not so much at the moment by direct action or a hurried approach. There are good reasons to sit back and take stock, and to think things through very carefully at every turn today. The planets are also supportive at the moment for speaking of love.

21 WEDNESDAY
Moon Age Day 9   Moon Sign Sagittarius

Today the spotlight is on your ability to communicate your ideas in a straightforward and no-nonsense sort of way, though this doesn't mean you have to be in any way abrupt. If you leave others in no doubt as to the way you feel about situations, there shouldn't be any confusion. Being precise is the surest key towards significant gains at present.

22 THURSDAY
Moon Age Day 10   Moon Sign Sagittarius

All manner of group activities are especially well starred today under the influence of the planet Mercury. You should easily be able to adapt your nature to suit changing circumstances, and needn't be fazed if you have to think on your feet. This would be a fantastic time to take a journey in the company of interesting folk.

23 FRIDAY
Moon Age Day 11   Moon Sign Sagittarius

Make the most of today by focusing on your social life and concentrating on letting your romantic partner know just how important they are to you. You have what it takes to be incredibly poetic, and sweeping people off their feet, even when you don't intend to do so, should be easy. It's time to keep life straightforward for the moment.

24 SATURDAY
Moon Age Day 12   Moon Sign Capricorn

Even if you are making sure things work out generally well in relationships, there is just a possibility you could find your love life to be slightly less than fulfilling. This is a response to your twelfth-house Venus, and you may find it extremely difficult to put your finger on what is wrong. In truth, it's possible that nothing is!

25 SUNDAY   *Moon Age Day 13   Moon Sign Capricorn*

Now is an ideal time to re-examine your emotional nature and to address any issues that have been buried below the surface. A good heart-to-heart talk with someone you trust would be no bad thing, and would be a chance to unburden yourself of anything that has been bugging you for a while. Once you have spoken out you should feel better.

26 MONDAY   *Moon Age Day 14   Moon Sign Aquarius*

The key today is to put a greater emphasis on leisure pursuits and on having a good time away from your usual responsibilities. This means that those Librans who have chosen this particular week to take their holidays have picked a very favourable time. Even if you are not on vacation, it's worth finding a few hours to do something exciting.

27 TUESDAY   *Moon Age Day 15   Moon Sign Aquarius*

The present planetary configuration encourages a more relaxed approach, and that means you probably needn't push yourself too hard. Have you managed to get ahead of yourself as far as work and general responsibilities are concerned? If so, you can probably afford to take some time out to do whatever takes your fancy.

28 WEDNESDAY   *Moon Age Day 16   Moon Sign Aquarius*

Remember that emotional issues that you may have been avoiding could well catch up with you, and that could mean having to face a serious conversation of some sort. This may not altogether please you at the moment because there is something quite superficial about your usually concerned nature. Try to keep it light and airy if you can.

29 THURSDAY   *Moon Age Day 17   Moon Sign Pisces*

Consistency seems to be the best route to personal success at this stage of the week, and you may well find that you get yourself into a fix if you jump about from one job to another. A sense of proportion is also necessary, but this might be more difficult to achieve at a time when excitement seems to be the name of the game.

119

30 FRIDAY   *Moon Age Day 18   Moon Sign Pisces*

The emphasis is on groups and associations of one sort or another and on the part they play in your life. Your best approach today is to surround yourself with as many people as possible. With everything to play for in terms of general good luck, you can afford to chance your arm more than you usually might.

31 SATURDAY   *Moon Age Day 19   Moon Sign Aries*

You would be wise to slow things down for the weekend, and this is hardly likely to be a bad thing given the presence of the lunar low. You can find your greatest pleasures in simple activities and the focus is on the support you give to others, rather than making the running yourself. Today isn't about moving around a great deal.

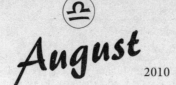

August 2010

1 SUNDAY
Moon Age Day 20   Moon Sign Aries

Ambitious schemes are best put on the back burner for the moment while you allow yourself the right to defer your judgement about almost anything until another day. You can push as hard as you like whilst the Moon is in its present position, but it might be difficult to make any significant headway. Sticking to what you know should work a treat.

2 MONDAY
Moon Age Day 21   Moon Sign Aries

In your personal life there could be the odd tricky situation to deal with today. You will need to take quick and intelligent action if you are to avoid giving offence where none is really intended. With the lunar low out of the way later in the day you can ensure things settle down, and it shouldn't be necessary for you to be quite so sensitive.

3 TUESDAY
Moon Age Day 22   Moon Sign Taurus

A day to display a ground-breaking and innovative attitude. New ideas can be given the green light and you should be able to inspire other people with the way you get on with things. Mars now in your solar first house assists you to overcome challenges as they arise, though that doesn't necessarily mean you have to actually go out and look for them!

4 WEDNESDAY
Moon Age Day 23   Moon Sign Taurus

In a social sense the emphasis is on the positive things that are taking place, and trends also highlight your wanderlust at present, which is enhanced by the summer weather. This should be an excellent time to inspire a little excitement in your life and to get family members and friends to let their hair down, even those who are usually quite reticent.

5 THURSDAY   *Moon Age Day 24   Moon Sign Gemini*

There are times when Libran subjects prefer a degree of fantasy instead of the real world, and that could occasionally be the case at the moment. Although Mars assists you to remain generally focused, little Mercury in your solar twelfth house supports unrealistic expectations and an inclination on your part to hope for the best.

6 FRIDAY   *Moon Age Day 25   Moon Sign Gemini*

If things stand still today you could find yourself getting very restless and inclined to jump about from foot to foot. For this reason your best approach is to be proactive and to try to make things happen. That's all very well, though you need to be careful if you are pushing other people into situations that would not normally be of their own choosing.

7 SATURDAY   *Moon Age Day 26   Moon Sign Cancer*

You now have scope to make great improvements in your love life, and you shouldn't find it remotely difficult to impress others with your attitude and generally warm nature. Your sense of fun is well accented around at this time, assisting you to achieve warm and humorous relationships with the people who always tend to inspire you the most.

8 SUNDAY   *Moon Age Day 27   Moon Sign Cancer*

This is a day for inspiration and creativity in equal quantities. You have what it takes to get things done and to inspire those around you – which is always a good sign. The only slight potential problem could be a tendency towards fuzzy thinking, so it is important to make certain that you remain focused on whatever you are doing.

9 MONDAY   *Moon Age Day 28   Moon Sign Leo*

Trends indicate something of a conflict between your own desires and the hopes and wishes of those with whom you live your life. Being a giving sort of person is fine, though there are occasions when your own ideas need to take centre stage. If you have confidence in your own thought processes, now is the time to follow them through.

122

10 TUESDAY
Moon Age Day 0   Moon Sign Leo

Erratic behaviour and an urge to be independent can both be legacies of the position of Mars in your solar chart around this time. You may be inclined to ignore your own instincts and to abandon something that has been working very well for you for some time. By all means be aware of 'alternatives', but don't necessarily opt for them without thinking.

11 WEDNESDAY
Moon Age Day 1   Moon Sign Virgo

This is probably not the best day of the month for getting out and about, though you can ensure that anything else you already had planned goes ahead as you expect. The Moon is now in your solar twelfth house, encouraging you to be more of a home bird. This would be a great time for pottering about in the garden, or even for sunbathing!

12 THURSDAY
Moon Age Day 2   Moon Sign Virgo

There is much to be said now for turning people who have merely been acquaintances in the past into friends. Your strength lies in your ability to be on good terms with just about everyone, and that might mean putting yourself out to accommodate different ideas and opinions. Fortunately this shouldn't be difficult for the average Libra-born individual.

13 FRIDAY
Moon Age Day 3   Moon Sign Libra

The best way to approach the world today is head-on. The lunar high offers you all the incentives you could possible need and encourages you to be positively explosive with ideas. There needn't be anything unlucky about this Friday the thirteenth as far as you are concerned, and success is there for the taking throughout the day.

14 SATURDAY
Moon Age Day 4   Moon Sign Libra

You can now make full use of your skills by implementing necessary changes to your normal routines, and you may decide you don't want to sit around and think too much under present trends. On the contrary, great satisfaction can be gained through making the running and doing what you can to persuade others to follow your lead.

15 SUNDAY
Moon Age Day 5   Moon Sign Libra

The lunar high is still around at the start of today, and taken together with that first-house Mars it remains a potent symbol of your determination and your positive attitude to life generally. There should be nothing 'standard' about you at the moment, and you can display the original, inspiring and funny side of your nature to everyone.

16 MONDAY
Moon Age Day 6   Moon Sign Scorpio

The present position of Venus in your solar chart supports a considerate and kind approach. It occupies your solar first house, and since it is your ruling planet this turns out to be extremely important. Make the most of the compliments you can attract from others, particularly concerning your appearance. After all, there's nothing wrong with looking good.

17 TUESDAY
Moon Age Day 7   Moon Sign Scorpio

Communications should be at the top of your list of priorities today, and it might be especially important to make the best of impressions on those with whom you work. As far as your home circumstances are concerned there are good reasons to consider switching things around and trying out different ways of organising yourself.

18 WEDNESDAY
Moon Age Day 8   Moon Sign Sagittarius

You can be a real battler at the moment and you should thrive on any sort of competition. There is a restless streak about that is best dealt with by movement and continued activity. Don't be hard on yourself if you can't get everything absolutely right first time. Everyone has to learn, and starting new things is always going to be a challenge.

19 THURSDAY
Moon Age Day 9   Moon Sign Sagittarius

You can afford to reserve some time today for celebrating and enjoying yourself. The spotlight is on important love relationships and you have what it takes to make the best possible impression on someone who has been, and remains, central to your thinking. Being a loner shouldn't be an option now, and sociability is the key.

20 FRIDAY   *Moon Age Day 10   Moon Sign Capricorn*

Don't waste any time that you spend at home today. The Moon is in your solar fourth house, assisting you to be more aware of the needs of family members. This would be an ideal time to sort things out on their behalf and also to dream up some new and imaginative ways to keep everyone happy and content.

21 SATURDAY   ☿ *Moon Age Day 11   Moon Sign Capricorn*

This is definitely not the best time for concentration and logic. Several planets are conspiring to support an active and reactive interlude, and a deep-thinking approach may not be as easy as would normally be the case. Today is about the 'immediate' and about responding positively to anything that sounds as though it might be exciting.

22 SUNDAY   ☿ *Moon Age Day 12   Moon Sign Capricorn*

Look for things to get excited about as far as your love life is concerned, and do all you can to pep things up in that particular area. You also have scope to show how charming and inspirational you can be as far as people beyond your emotional life are concerned. Finding that you have secret admirers isn't out of the question now.

23 MONDAY   ☿ *Moon Age Day 13   Moon Sign Aquarius*

With Mars in your solar first house a more argumentative approach may be a natural aspect of life now. You needn't allow this to be the case when you are dealing with people you know well, but authority figures could easily get on your nerves and you might find it especially difficult to deal with red tape.

24 TUESDAY   ☿ *Moon Age Day 14   Moon Sign Aquarius*

You have potential to be significantly more intuitive than usual, and can use this trait in a number of different ways. By all means focus on home and family if you can, though if you are committed to being out there in the wider world all day you should still be able to find little periods when you can relax. Remember that too much mental concentration can be tiring.

25 WEDNESDAY ☿   *Moon Age Day 15   Moon Sign Pisces*

Ensuring that you are ready for new plans and quite revolutionary schemes is very important. It might be better not to embark on anything out of the ordinary unless you have worked out your strategies first, because present trends do not assist you to think on your feet as well as would usually be the case for a Libran individual.

26 THURSDAY   ☿   *Moon Age Day 16   Moon Sign Pisces*

Conservative ideas are not for you at this time, and the emphasis is on being quite radical in your approach to almost anything. People who are used to your kind and gentle ways might be slightly surprised to see how reactive and assertive you are capable of being. With Mars in its present position, you might even surprise yourself!

27 FRIDAY   ☿   *Moon Age Day 17   Moon Sign Pisces*

The lunar low comes along tomorrow and since it could be quite potent it would be sensible to get anything important out of the way now. Leave yourself free for some sort of retreat into your own shell and also consider doing some delegating today so that you can afford to take some time out tomorrow. Act like a boy scout – be prepared.

28 SATURDAY   ☿   *Moon Age Day 18   Moon Sign Aries*

Communication may not be all you would wish today, and getting hold of the wrong end of the stick is a distinct possibility. Where details are concerned it would be sensible to check and check again in order to ensure that something important is not missed. A lunar low at the weekend generally supports a quieter social period.

29 SUNDAY   ☿   *Moon Age Day 19   Moon Sign Aries*

Slower-moving trends are working through at present, though there are some strong underlying planetary positions. As a result you could feel somewhat frustrated when things don't turn out as you might have wished. On the one hand there are influences encouraging a forceful and determined approach, but on the other you may simply want to relax.

30 MONDAY ☿ *Moon Age Day 20   Moon Sign Taurus*

There could now be slightly less interest in the social world and a greater focus on your own inner self. What you do for others in a concrete sense remains important, though you needn't be quite so determined to run the show when you are amongst friends. This is potentially a day for enjoyment, but what form it takes is up to you.

31 TUESDAY ☿ *Moon Age Day 21   Moon Sign Taurus*

Under the influence of Mars you may well say things you will come to regret, so it is vitally important to monitor your speech and avoid speaking out about anything that is a major issue to you. Better by far to keep silent for the moment than to give the sort of offence that will take you weeks or months to counter. Strengthen your finances now.

September
2010

1 WEDNESDAY ☿ *Moon Age Day 22 Moon Sign Gemini*

It's the first day of September and the Sun is in your solar twelfth house. This heralds a more spiritual time and encourages you to turn away from physical experiences towards more ethereal ones. Keep in tune with your senses because they are unlikely to lead you astray, and it looks as though your intuition will be your best guide for a while.

2 THURSDAY ☿ *Moon Age Day 23 Moon Sign Gemini*

A day to keep in contact with a variety of alternative sorts of people, especially those from different walks of life. Life can be quite rewarding, though if you are displaying the deeper side of your nature you may be somewhat difficult for others to fathom. Actually this can be an advantage, because the harder you are to read, the more attractive you can be.

3 FRIDAY ☿ *Moon Age Day 24 Moon Sign Cancer*

You now have scope to seek a great deal of reassurance from the direction of family members, and there are positive trends associated with being close to home, both today and across the weekend. This doesn't mean you should restrict yourself in any way, and nor does it infer you that have to be particularly quiet.

4 SATURDAY ☿ *Moon Age Day 25 Moon Sign Cancer*

By all means back your ambition with a determination to get things done, but what really counts is the method you choose. The Sun supports a contemplative and spiritual approach, but Mars urges you forward aggressively. Between the two is a path towards achievement and even success. All you have to do is to find it!

5 SUNDAY   ☿   *Moon Age Day 26   Moon Sign Leo*

Don't look for a means of escape today if you feel threatened in some way. You have what it takes to look demons clear in the face and you can win out, even in situations that might make you nervous. Getting what you want from your lover should be easy, and it would be simplicity itself to settle for romance and little else at this time.

6 MONDAY   ☿   *Moon Age Day 27   Moon Sign Leo*

The present position of Venus is favourable for your emotional state and encourages a placid and easy-going approach. There's nothing strange about that for Libra and you can display yourself at the moment as being fairly typical of your zodiac sign. Any strong intuitive insights should not be ignored under current influences.

7 TUESDAY   ☿   *Moon Age Day 28   Moon Sign Leo*

You can now afford to forego your own desires and wishes on account of your hopes for those around you. This is particularly true in terms of your lover, so don't be afraid to go to great lengths at the moment for those you care about the most. Even if you can't get everyone on your side, especially at work, you should be able to convince those who matter.

8 WEDNESDAY   ☿   *Moon Age Day 0   Moon Sign Virgo*

Now is the time to push hard towards whatever goals are uppermost in your mind at the moment, and you have what it takes to keep going when others have fallen by the wayside. Some of your personal ambitions could be at odds with your family concerns, but there is always a middle path to follow and Librans are usually good at finding it.

9 THURSDAY   ☿   *Moon Age Day 1   Moon Sign Virgo*

A slightly quieter interlude is possible today, but that needn't prevent you from getting where you want to be under most circumstances. Your best approach is not to make a great fuss about anything you do at present, and that assists you to attract help from those around you. In some ways you might even be playing for the sympathy vote.

129

10 FRIDAY ☿ *Moon Age Day 2   Moon Sign Libra*

Professional matters are the ones that are really well accented during this particular lunar high. However, you have the opportunity to be on top form in terms of your social impulses too, and can use this to associate with as many different people as proves to be possible. Routines are for the birds today, so why not avoid them?

11 SATURDAY ☿ *Moon Age Day 3   Moon Sign Libra*

Today is about your ability to express yourself and to get others to follow your lead without any difficulty at all. Getting out of the house and doing something different is the name of the game this weekend. Make the most of the luck that is available, perhaps by opting for a shopping spree in the hope of finding some bargains.

12 SUNDAY ☿ *Moon Age Day 4   Moon Sign Scorpio*

There's nothing wrong with seeking a little solitude today, but whatever you decide to do, it's worth being more contemplative and less inclined to push yourself forward. Everyone needs thinking time, and Libra is no different in this regard. It's time to make detailed plans for your next move, either at work or in a particular relationship.

13 MONDAY ☿ *Moon Age Day 5   Moon Sign Scorpio*

If there is any disappointment to be dealt with today, you have what it takes to carry on regardless and to get through any problems that do arise. There are good reasons to find time to get in touch with people you don't see too often and to be as bold as possible when it comes to letting others know what you think are your rights.

14 TUESDAY *Moon Age Day 6   Moon Sign Sagittarius*

Short trips taken at this time can be therapeutic and can offer you a different sort of insight into any issues that have puzzled you of late. Valuable information is there for you to use to your advantage, and you really need to take notice of all the little messages that you become aware of at this time. Look for new experiences later in the day.

15 WEDNESDAY   *Moon Age Day 7   Moon Sign Sagittarius*

You now have scope to bring stability to financial matters and to put yourself in the driving seat when it comes to professional plans. An unsettled period is possible at home, and your best approach to resolving this is to take the people concerned on one side and talk things through with them.

16 THURSDAY   *Moon Age Day 8   Moon Sign Capricorn*

Trends suggest you may find yourself preoccupied with a personal, emotional matter at some stage today. Rather than dwelling on things, you need to draw your present experiences from as large a cross-section of life as you can manage. By turning your attention outwards you may come to understand the answers that evade you when you think too deeply.

17 FRIDAY   *Moon Age Day 9   Moon Sign Capricorn*

Your imagination is stimulated best if you remain in touch with others. Though there is nothing at all surprising about this for a Libran subject, your contacts with the world at large are even more important than ever right now. This isn't a day to keep quiet if you have something to crow about as far as your love life is concerned!

18 SATURDAY   *Moon Age Day 10   Moon Sign Capricorn*

Now you have a natural ability to express yourself and to handle your emotions in a reasoned and adult way. But can the same be said to be the case for everyone close to you? If certain people aren't handling their own disappointments in life at all well, this would be an ideal time to find some way to sort them out.

19 SUNDAY   *Moon Age Day 11   Moon Sign Aquarius*

Your acquisitive tendencies are now to the fore, encouraging you to gather all sorts of things around you that you really don't need at all. This runs counter to some of the most powerful planetary influences surrounding you at present, most of which are urging you to lighten your load and to dump anything irrelevant.

20 MONDAY · Moon Age Day 12 · Moon Sign Aquarius

There's nothing wrong with being influenced by other people and their ideas. This could well be the case at the moment, though you needn't simply take their schemes on board – rather, you can use your skills to modify and improve them. What this does for your personal popularity remains to be seen, but that shouldn't hold you back.

21 TUESDAY · Moon Age Day 13 · Moon Sign Pisces

When it comes to the emotional side of your life, trends assist you to be on top form and to show yourself at your very best. Be prepared to make the most of romantic overtures, perhaps from some quite unexpected directions, and avoid creating any jealousy around you by making a special fuss of your really important person.

22 WEDNESDAY · Moon Age Day 14 · Moon Sign Pisces

A phase of introspection is on offer, and you can afford to be quieter as the lunar low approaches. This doesn't mean you have to stop trying or that you need to retreat absolutely into your own shell. Rather, it's a chance to consider situations more carefully and to avoid having to make rash decisions on the spur of the moment.

23 THURSDAY · Moon Age Day 15 · Moon Sign Pisces

Today works best if you remain essentially steady and a little more introspective than might normally be the case for a typical Libran. All the same you can make progress, and in some ways to a greater extent than normal. A day to focus your mind and see things in stark contrast, without getting yourself mixed up with too many peripheral matters.

24 FRIDAY · Moon Age Day 16 · Moon Sign Aries

It might be difficult now to make solid choices. With the lunar low really having a bearing on your life today and tomorrow you would be wise to seek some sound advice from your friends and especially your partner. Don't be afraid to let others make the running, whilst you sit back and, if necessary, supervise.

25 SATURDAY   *Moon Age Day 17   Moon Sign Aries*

Rather than depending on big plans today, why not use the first part of the weekend to think things through carefully and slowly? You may decide you don't want to socialise as much as you often do at the weekend, but there is much to be said for spending time in the bosom of your family. Even household chores might now seem inviting!

26 SUNDAY   *Moon Age Day 18   Moon Sign Taurus*

A time of potential change in your social life, though this may not all be inspiring. Remember that it's natural for people to move around and for groups to change over time. In the end your best response is to try to see the positive side of whatever is taking place around you at the moment, and to make the best of every situation.

27 MONDAY   *Moon Age Day 19   Moon Sign Taurus*

Certain complexities could be making your life more difficult, and you may need to face choices that you don't really want to address at all. If you have to do something you haven't been looking forward to doing, it would be best to get it out of the way early in the day. That way you leave yourself free to find fun later on.

28 TUESDAY   *Moon Age Day 20   Moon Sign Taurus*

Your independent, pioneering spirit should definitely be on display now. The Sun has now entered your solar first house and this assists you to make the most of two or three of the best weeks of the year so far, especially in terms of the progress you can make in a material sense. If you know what looks and feels right at present, stick to it.

29 WEDNESDAY   *Moon Age Day 21   Moon Sign Gemini*

This could be an ideal opportunity for a trip or a vacation of some sort, and though this may come as a surprise you need to react as positively and quickly as you can. A change of venue could help you to release any tensions you have been feeling in the recent past, and to slow your mind down from its present frenetic pace.

133

30 THURSDAY   *Moon Age Day 22   Moon Sign Gemini*

Mars has now moved on in your chart and no longer occupies its first-house position. This allows you to be more considered in your thinking and actions and also to be calmer within yourself than you might have been for months. Today is also about using your strong enthusiasm for monetary matters and thinking up some good ideas.

October

2010

1 FRIDAY
Moon Age Day 23   Moon Sign Cancer

Positive changes are now possible as far as your monetary fortunes are concerned. It could be in your interest to focus on investments at this time and to think carefully about ways in which you can make whatever money you do have grow. Even if certain luxury items are now easier to come by, ask yourself whether you really need them.

2 SATURDAY
Moon Age Day 24   Moon Sign Cancer

You have what it takes to improve your standing in group situations and to impress others, particularly anyone you see as being a role model. Actually it isn't a question of trying really hard if popularity is what you are seeking. It is available all the time for Libra, assisting you to remain high in the estimation of many of those you know.

3 SUNDAY
Moon Age Day 25   Moon Sign Leo

Your self-determining approach to life is highlighted at the moment, which it ought to be with a first-house Sun. You needn't take other people's word for anything if it is possible for you to try things out for yourself. There is financial progress to be made now and across the coming days, and a positive attitude can work wonders!

4 MONDAY
Moon Age Day 26   Moon Sign Leo

An ideal day for socialising, though there may be difficulties to deal with. Ask yourself whether these have arisen because you are very sure of your ground at the moment and refuse to be bamboozled by others in any way. There are ways and means of getting what you want today, and simple confrontation is not the best one.

5 TUESDAY
Moon Age Day 27   Moon Sign Virgo

If everyday life is beset with small problems, you have what it takes to overcome these quite easily. Any frustrations that do come along are best addressed one at a time, perhaps with the assistance of colleagues or friends. Try not to allow life to become too complicated and wherever possible stick to what you know well.

6 WEDNESDAY
Moon Age Day 28   Moon Sign Virgo

With Venus in its present position you have an opportunity to attract the finer things in life to a greater extent. Your natural sense of poise is emphasised, assisting you to exude that famous charm that sets Libra apart. Because of this the attention you can attract from others should be positive, and you can use it to get others on board with your plans.

7 THURSDAY
Moon Age Day 29   Moon Sign Libra

Be prepared to deal with changes of direction today and to act at a moment's notice when opportunities come your way. It's a question of using the energy that is available and showing your determination to a greater extent than has been the case for a while. Lady Luck shines on you during the lunar high, so make the most of the fact.

8 FRIDAY
Moon Age Day 0   Moon Sign Libra

Events now reach a high watermark, because in addition to the lunar high you can also take advantage of a first-house Sun. Together these influences indicate this to be the best time to make your move, especially at work. Socially speaking the key is to make sure you are the centre of attention and attraction. You can make this a very interesting day.

9 SATURDAY
Moon Age Day 1   Moon Sign Scorpio

Bear in mind that not all your ideas may find favour with others at this time, and that you will have to work slightly harder than usual if you want to get the best from even personal situations. It could be that those around you are just being awkward, but you need to ask yourself whether they may have a point. Diplomacy works best now.

10 SUNDAY   *Moon Age Day 2   Moon Sign Scorpio*

Trends support a somewhat rash approach, which could lead to difficulties further down the line. Try to be circumspect and to think about eventualities before they actually come along. A little caution is important in your love life, because if you make bold statements you may be challenged to back them up in some way.

11 MONDAY   *Moon Age Day 3   Moon Sign Sagittarius*

Today should be positive for finance and also for developing the favourable impression you want to give to others. Being born of an Air sign you always have potential to fly high and to show great enthusiasm. Just at the moment you may be doing so to such an extent that you attract the sort of attention you probably don't need.

12 TUESDAY   *Moon Age Day 4   Moon Sign Sagittarius*

You now have an opportunity to make a significant amount of progress in a practical sense, though you may lose out slightly in the personality stakes. It could be difficult maintaining your popularity with some people in the face of actions you know you should take. Compromises are called for, so get your thinking cap on.

13 WEDNESDAY   *Moon Age Day 5   Moon Sign Sagittarius*

Your clever and quick mind can generally work to your advantage and today should be no exception. This is a time for new insights and for putting plans into action that have been at the back of your mind for quite some time. There is assistance on offer if you need it, so don't be too proud or to embarrassed to ask.

14 THURSDAY   *Moon Age Day 6   Moon Sign Capricorn*

You could be at odds today with anyone who doesn't have the same opinions as you do, perhaps regarding money and the way it should be either spent or saved. Once again it's time to use your natural diplomacy and turn on the charm in order to get what you want. Not all your decisions now will be easy, but you can ensure that they are honest.

15 FRIDAY
Moon Age Day 7   Moon Sign Capricorn

Your desire to succeed more and more is heightened whilst the Sun stays in your solar first house. You have what it takes to get things done in a practical sense and also to bring others round to your particular point of view. Don't be afraid to put yourself at the forefront of any major plans that are taking place around you.

16 SATURDAY
Moon Age Day 8   Moon Sign Aquarius

This would be a very good time to put your persuasive tongue to work at home, and this could make negotiations and discussions a piece of cake during the weekend. Today is about ensuring that your personal targets in life are now standing on firm ground, and using your patience and determination to the full.

17 SUNDAY
Moon Age Day 9   Moon Sign Aquarius

A break from your normal routines would be no bad thing on this particular day, especially if you have the free time to do whatever takes your fancy. You may decide you don't want to be doing anything alone at the moment because the sociable side of Libra is definitely emphasised. Whatever you do, take friends along with you.

18 MONDAY
Moon Age Day 10   Moon Sign Aquarius

You can afford to remain optimistic and confident at the start of a new working week, and should be able to put many of your present plans into words that those around you will fully understand. Telling a tale is never hard for you, but at the moment you can be quite poetic and inclined to sugar any pill to such an extent that it will seem like caviar!

19 TUESDAY
Moon Age Day 11   Moon Sign Pisces

A day to put lots of energy into getting what you want, not only for your own sake but on behalf of those you care for. If there is one aspect of your nature that is really finely tuned at present it is your 'balance', and this enhances your ability to see all sides of situations well in advance. Be prepared to get others to follow your lead now.

20 WEDNESDAY   *Moon Age Day 12   Moon Sign Pisces*

Even if you remain active and enterprising, you might be feeling the weight of some responsibilities, particularly ones you have take on board willingly. Maybe you didn't realise how much would be expected of you, but you shouldn't be afraid to seek some help if the going gets too tough. Support from colleagues and friends can really make a difference now.

21 THURSDAY   *Moon Age Day 13   Moon Sign Aries*

Frustrations are always a possibility while the lunar low pays its monthly visit, but these are likely to be fleeting and of no real consequence. It might be best not to take on too much for today or tomorrow and to give yourself the time you need to rest and relax. Whether or not you take this course of action is up to you, though it would be advantageous.

22 FRIDAY   *Moon Age Day 14   Moon Sign Aries*

There are good reasons to make this a lay-off period between adventures and to seek the comfort of your own hearth and home if possible. You have scope to get on especially well with family members at the moment and to create a good deal of joy in your love life. It may be more difficult to create amusement at the moment.

23 SATURDAY   *Moon Age Day 15   Moon Sign Aries*

As the Sun moves from your solar first house to the second, it's time to face up to new starts, altered opportunities and positive chance discoveries. Don't leave any stone unturned in your desire to know what makes things tick in the way they do. It's also important to keep on line and in tune with people who think in a similar way to you.

24 SUNDAY   *Moon Age Day 16   Moon Sign Taurus*

Trends assist you to feel slightly more secure about life because even if the last month has been busy and eventful, it might also have been a little precarious in some ways. This is an ideal time to solidify some of your schemes and to investigate opportunities to strengthen your finances more than has recently been the case.

139

25 MONDAY
Moon Age Day 17   Moon Sign Taurus

Attracting good things is a natural part of life for you now, and there is much to be said for keeping money at the forefront of your mind. Your best approach to attracting cash is to remain careful in your thinking and planning. You may also have a chance to bring to maturity some of your efforts from a much earlier stage.

26 TUESDAY
Moon Age Day 18   Moon Sign Gemini

Social interactions offer you the opportunity to keep on the go and to join in with group activities. Rather than being out there alone in the lead, your strength now lies in your willingness to share and to attribute any success you do have to your friends. Even if this is true in part, you shouldn't be so modest that you fail to recognise your own efforts.

27 WEDNESDAY
Moon Age Day 19   Moon Sign Gemini

You now have what it takes to make better use of your financial resources and to discover that you are slightly better off in some way than you expected to be. Little mishaps are possible today, but you should be able to turn at least some of these to your advantage. Mechanical things in particular could cause you some stress.

28 THURSDAY
Moon Age Day 20   Moon Sign Cancer

Even if you've managed to get finances looking a little rosier, relationships may be causing you one or two problems. The closer people are to you, the greater is the chance that they will misbehave or act in ways of which you do not approve. It would be far better to shrug off any little frustrations rather than reacting to them.

29 FRIDAY
Moon Age Day 21   Moon Sign Cancer

Now you have planetary influences that indicate professional gains and an even more forward-looking attitude on your part. Be prepared to get things finished off ahead of the weekend and don't leave anything flapping in the wind as far as work is concerned. That way you can get straight back into action on Monday and make instant progress.

30 SATURDAY   *Moon Age Day 22   Moon Sign Cancer*

The money area of your life is definitely activated by the present position of the Sun, and even if you aren't obsessed with finances, they could be of significance at the present time. Are relatives spending too much? This would be an ideal day to address the situation. If you do, keep your discussions as light-hearted as possible.

31 SUNDAY   *Moon Age Day 23   Moon Sign Leo*

Groups and friendship generally are well highlighted, indicating this to be a day that allows you to benefit from the involvement of others in your daily life. Trends encourage you to stay sociable and out there amidst your friends, and not to spend too much time sitting and ruminating. Activity is now the best tonic for any form of the blues.

November
2010

1 MONDAY
Moon Age Day 24   Moon Sign Leo

Planetary trends now abound with a beneficial focus on finance. You may have the chance to gamble a little, though it's not worth taking the sort of chances that could lead to major difficulties later. It's important to ensure your decisions are confident and considered, and this should help you to get others to follow your lead.

2 TUESDAY
Moon Age Day 25   Moon Sign Virgo

You have a particular talent for dealing with people and the fact is extremely well emphasised at the moment. Persuading those around you to conform to your will shouldn't be difficult, and you can even do it without them realising that anything of the sort is going on. Avoid unnecessary arguments at home today and stick to social ties if you can.

3 WEDNESDAY
Moon Age Day 26   Moon Sign Virgo

A slightly quieter approach works best today, this being a very temporary state of affairs that is supported by the position of the Moon. The emphasis is on thinking things through carefully, and you may not be quite as gregarious as you have been recently. You can change all this tomorrow if you decide to throw caution to the wind.

4 THURSDAY
Moon Age Day 27   Moon Sign Libra

The lunar high is a good time for general progress and a period during which you can show yourself off to the best of your ability. It's a question of being aware of the way you look and of making the best impression you can on others. General good luck is there for the taking, so there's every reason to be extremely cheerful today.

5 FRIDAY
Moon Age Day 28   Moon Sign Libra

The high-energy phase continues as the lunar high works its magic around you. It might seem to be making others more amenable to your nature, though you need to consider whether in fact you are charming them into accepting your point of view. Romance is well starred, and it's time to make sure you are number one in the eyes of someone important.

6 SATURDAY
Moon Age Day 0   Moon Sign Scorpio

You can be so dynamic and forceful in your dealings with people generally that some of them may well get a definite shock. It isn't like you to be dominant, and you usually get what you want by using your charm. But trends now encourage you to cut to the chase in any situation, and you may not tolerate the stupidity of others very well.

7 SUNDAY
Moon Age Day 1   Moon Sign Scorpio

Today might drag somewhat, particularly if you are spending time dealing with the minutiae of life when what you really want to do is to spread your wings and fly. One option is to reorganise situations so that you have more time to do whatever appeals to you directly. Seeking help from others would be no bad thing later on.

8 MONDAY
Moon Age Day 2   Moon Sign Sagittarius

A new and beneficial period is on offer, especially when it comes to practical matters. This assists your efforts to get on well at work, and helps you to take advantage of opportunities for advancement or for some sort of honour. It's time to prove to yourself that you have been doing something right across the last few months.

9 TUESDAY
Moon Age Day 3   Moon Sign Sagittarius

You are always good at tuning in to the thoughts and emotions of others but this skill is even more accentuated under present trends. This allows you to second guess the way people around you are likely to behave and it can be a good incentive to being in the right place to benefit alongside them. Affairs of the heart are heavily accented.

10 WEDNESDAY   *Moon Age Day 4   Moon Sign Capricorn*

Lots of brand new input is on offer, and your communication skills could turn out to be a distinct advantage to you now. Your curiosity knows no bounds, and you should be willing to go to any lengths to find out things you see as being important. Some of the discoveries you make might be disquieting, but they are also likely to be exciting.

11 THURSDAY   *Moon Age Day 5   Moon Sign Capricorn*

Domestic issues are favourably highlighted around now, assisting you to achieve contentment and happiness as far as your home life is concerned. If there are any unsettling moments, these may well emerge in your social life. Ask yourself whether you are being forced to take the blame for someone else's problems.

12 FRIDAY   *Moon Age Day 6   Moon Sign Capricorn*

Finances are well starred, encouraging you to let investments run their course. You may not panic about money, but on the other hand you may be thrown off course in terms of romance. Maybe someone is saying the wrong thing or taking a course of action you don't understand. The best way forward is to ask for an explanation.

13 SATURDAY   *Moon Age Day 7   Moon Sign Aquarius*

You are now in a position to make a strong impact on your surroundings, especially at home. If you are in any way uncomfortable with your domestic arrangements, now is the time to alter them, well ahead of the Christmas period. It could simply be a change in the furniture or else something far more fundamental. It's worth seeking other family opinions.

14 SUNDAY   *Moon Age Day 8   Moon Sign Aquarius*

If your usual diplomatic talents aren't quite so obvious for the moment, for this you can thank the presence of Mars in your solar third house. This planetary position supports a slightly less patient approach to communication than would normally be the case, and makes this a time when you may be much less likely to suffer fools gladly.

15 MONDAY
Moon Age Day 9   Moon Sign Pisces

You can now afford to be more ambitious and to use your clout to back up your wishes for the future. In a professional sense this might take you as close to being ruthless as Libra ever gets – but even this is far short of some of the people surrounding you. Nevertheless, it's time to make an impression and forge a new path.

16 TUESDAY
Moon Age Day 10   Moon Sign Pisces

Trends indicate you might have your work cut out at present if you really want to prosper and to get ahead, though this needn't be any sort of problem. It's all a question of channelling your energy and courage into taking those steps you see as being important. Avoid being too judgemental today regarding the lives of your friends.

17 WEDNESDAY
Moon Age Day 11   Moon Sign Aries

All of a sudden you are urged to slow things down to a snail's pace, at least as far as your professional and practical life is concerned. The lunar low can bring you to a virtual standstill, but you needn't allow it to shake your resolve. Instead of actually doing things for the next couple of days, your best response is to plan your next moves.

18 THURSDAY
Moon Age Day 12   Moon Sign Aries

A day to put major issues and decisions on the back burner and enjoy watching what is happening around you. It is impossible for you to take part in everything, even if you feel as though you should be doing just that. Matters of the heart respond best if you are gentle, understanding and quite willing to listen to an alternative point of view.

19 FRIDAY
Moon Age Day 13   Moon Sign Aries

Venus is now in your solar first house and this can act as something of an antidote to that third-house Mars. What does this mean? Well, it assists you to be two people in one, because with those you love you can show your warm and sympathetic side, but if you are out there in the wider world you can display a far more assertive face.

20 SATURDAY · *Moon Age Day 14 · Moon Sign Taurus*

The things you say today may well clash with the opinions of people you normally get on with extremely well. It might be impossible to change the situation, but you should at least realise that people don't always see eye-to-eye and leave it at that. Constantly analysing what individuals say may not be the best use of your time at the moment.

21 SUNDAY · *Moon Age Day 15 · Moon Sign Taurus*

Personal and emotional ambitions can be brought to a head around now, and there are good reasons to spend time putting the finishing touches to specific plans. Newer and better ways of expressing yourself are also possible, maybe because of the change of heart of someone close to you. Keep a firm hand on the tiller of your finances now.

22 MONDAY · *Moon Age Day 16 · Moon Sign Gemini*

You can now be at your mental best, with sharp insights and an instinctive understanding of how to behave under any given circumstance. Not everyone around you might be equally helpful, and some impatience would be a natural response if others failed to match your expectations. Libra's normal patience may be hard to find at present.

23 TUESDAY · *Moon Age Day 17 · Moon Sign Gemini*

Making progress is easier if you maintain connections and keep in touch with people who you know can be important to your longer-term success. If these are individuals you don't care for very much, you may decide to be a little duplicitous and pretend you like them. Even your most selfish thoughts can be directed to serving the greater good.

24 WEDNESDAY · *Moon Age Day 18 · Moon Sign Gemini*

Quick answers, a great wit and a sense of humour that knows no bounds. All these are gifts that you should put on full display under present trends. Remember that it's a fine line between this side of your nature and a cutting and even sarcastic approach. Nobody can doubt that you have an 'edge', and you can use this to get people to look in your direction.

25 THURSDAY   *Moon Age Day 19   Moon Sign Cancer*

Any personal doubts about the general progress of your life should now be thrown out of the window as you push on towards your chosen destinations in life. If routines are a real chore at the moment, why not look for ways to avoid as many of them as you can? In personal matters there ought to be room for a new approach and some tenderness.

26 FRIDAY   *Moon Age Day 20   Moon Sign Cancer*

You have what it takes to communicate with consummate skill, though there is nothing especially strange about that for a Libran. What can really make all the difference is how well acquainted you are with the way those around you are thinking. This allows you to take the right actions to keep both you and them as happy as could be.

27 SATURDAY   *Moon Age Day 21   Moon Sign Leo*

Involvement with groups is emphasised at this time, assisting you to get on much better with people en masse than you are likely to do with specific individuals. You have a chance to elicit interesting information from almost everyone you meet at the moment, and some of the things you learn could well be of practical use later on.

28 SUNDAY   *Moon Age Day 22   Moon Sign Leo*

Another ideal day for meet exciting people and for learning a great deal about yourself and your own life as a result. By constantly making comparisons you can move forward progressively and improve your reservoir of knowledge on the way. This isn't a favourable time for making binding commitments, particularly if you are not sure.

29 MONDAY   *Moon Age Day 23   Moon Sign Virgo*

By all means try as hard as you can to make specific individuals understand what you are trying to tell them, especially if you think the importance of what you are saying is being lost in the complications of life. Even if you have to reinforce your views time and again, this is the best way of ensuring in the end that you have done everything possible.

30 TUESDAY
Moon Age Day 24   Moon Sign Virgo

Today's influences assist you to derive a great deal of satisfaction from the seemingly endless social round of which you are a part. There is much to be said for taking on board the opinions of friends, though some family members could be giving you problems. As is often the case for Libra, a complicated life can also be interesting.

December

2010

1 WEDNESDAY
Moon Age Day 25   Moon Sign Libra

It's worth testing out ideas with regard to their ultimate feasibility before you get yourself too deeply involved in them. Many inventive solutions to old problems are available under the lunar high, so now is the time to focus your ingenious and practical mind. Even if not everyone likes you at the moment, you can make sure that the people who matter do.

2 THURSDAY
Moon Age Day 26   Moon Sign Libra

Expansive new opportunities are now within your grasp, and there seems to be no end to your ingenuity and appeal. Your popularity shouldn't be in doubt, particularly if you continue to show how considerate of others you really are. Even so, that third-house Mars is still around, emphasising the more aggressive side of your nature.

3 FRIDAY
Moon Age Day 27   Moon Sign Scorpio

You can now be extremely powerful when it comes to putting across your point of view, but people shouldn't mind as long as you remain fair and open-minded. Where you could come unstuck is if you are determined to dominate conversations or show how dismissive you can be regarding a plan of action that isn't your own.

4 SATURDAY
Moon Age Day 28   Moon Sign Scorpio

The weekend is a chance for you to make progress on the financial front, and you seem to have what it takes to make a greater material success of your life at this time. This is also a favourable time for pursuing a busy social life, and there is much to be said for handing out invitations for impromptu gatherings that others can come along and enjoy.

5 SUNDAY
Moon Age Day 29   Moon Sign Sagittarius

You can now be at your best when you surround yourself with your favourite people, though you may not have that much time for those you don't care for. As a general rule you can cover up your animosity, but to do so may be more difficult at present. Life is all about attitude, and yours can be just a little suspect under present planetary trends.

6 MONDAY
Moon Age Day 0   Moon Sign Sagittarius

This ought to be a day of great inspiration. You really do have a lot going for you at present and there are gains to be made in several different areas of your life. As far as meetings and agreements are concerned, today could prove to be very favourable, though it's still worth keeping an eye out for the odd awkward friend.

7 TUESDAY
Moon Age Day 1   Moon Sign Capricorn

At home it will be better to offer support today than to expect it to be coming your way. Seeking help from other people might actually end up making small problems worse. The dependable side of your nature is still to the fore, and you can demonstrate this to your nearest and dearest. Don't forget to spend some time on yourself if possible.

8 WEDNESDAY
Moon Age Day 2   Moon Sign Capricorn

Venus is still in your solar second house and this offers you scope to achieve greater financial stability and to line up your resources in a more logical and useful way. Love is well marked, and this would be an ideal time for those Libran subjects who are between attachments to get out and make the most of romantic opportunities.

9 THURSDAY
Moon Age Day 3   Moon Sign Capricorn

Trends suggest that making an impact on people who are in a position to do you some good has surely never been easier than turns out to be the case right now. It's time to strike while the iron is hot and to make your feelings known right across the spectrum of your life. If you can persuade people to listen to what you have to say, they should react positively.

10 FRIDAY   *Moon Age Day 4   Moon Sign Aquarius*

It's important to leave more space for the emotions of those around you. Although you might think you feel strongly about certain issues, there may be other people who become far more emotionally stretched than you. Being caring and understanding is a great part of what you naturally are, and the fact really does need to show today.

11 SATURDAY   ☿ *Moon Age Day 5   Moon Sign Aquarius*

There's nothing wrong with having people relying on your opinions – in fact, a whole variety of people may be doing so at the moment. It might be something as simple as advice about what to buy at the shops, or else an issue that is far more serious, but whatever you are called upon to comment on today will be important to somebody, so be totally honest.

12 SUNDAY   ☿   *Moon Age Day 6   Moon Sign Pisces*

A variety of interests will help you to get the most from life at this time and this particular Sunday has potential to be especially good in terms of the social scene. Are you already gearing up for the festive season? There are strong home-based trends at work, so getting the decorations out might be the order of the day!

13 MONDAY   ☿   *Moon Age Day 7   Moon Sign Pisces*

The critical side of your nature is emphasised, and in domestic encounters this might mean you cause offence without realising you are doing so. As a rule you tread very carefully on other people's sensibilities, but you may not be quite as sensitive as would usually be the case. Be prepared to bite your tongue before you react harshly right now.

14 TUESDAY   ☿   *Moon Age Day 8   Moon Sign Pisces*

A potentially quieter spell arrives tomorrow, but for the moment you should still have sufficient drive and determination to finish off jobs and to get your head round what lies before you. Frustrations are possible, particularly in terms of the practical side of life, which is about to be overtaken by a dose of 'impending Christmas disease'.

15 WEDNESDAY ☿   *Moon Age Day 9   Moon Sign Aries*

It may now be difficult to make use of your energy and vitality, and the lunar low could well take the wind from your sails when it comes to practical progress. There's nothing wrong with being content with half measures or leaving some jobs until later. Making excuses isn't ideal, but in some situations there may be very little choice but to do so.

16 THURSDAY ☿   *Moon Age Day 10   Moon Sign Aries*

If you feel your powers are limited, you may decide to call upon the good offices of friends and colleagues. There is no shame in this, and you have what it takes to persuade people to lend you a hand, particularly if they realise how much you do for others. Despite any problems today, you can afford to remain essentially optimistic.

17 FRIDAY ☿   *Moon Age Day 11   Moon Sign Taurus*

Your strength lies in your ability to deal with pressures from the outside world and with a busier pace of life. At least the lunar low is out of the way, offering you a chance to get involved in new projects. There may be some obstacles around, particularly if those upon whom you rely won't come up with the goods.

18 SATURDAY ☿   *Moon Age Day 12   Moon Sign Taurus*

The Sun is presently in your third house of communications, assisting you to get your message across in almost any situation. By all means be quite careful not to stand on the sensibilities of other people, though you might also need to be fairly direct. Today is about how you tread this fine line.

19 SUNDAY ☿   *Moon Age Day 13   Moon Sign Taurus*

Trends encourage you to do something completely different today, and it's worth seeking the support of any of your friends who are as bored by convention as you are. Socially speaking you should be on top form, and the lure of the Christmas season is now fully upon you. Duties will probably be far less inviting than adventures at this stage.

20 MONDAY ☿ *Moon Age Day 14   Moon Sign Gemini*

A more enriched period is now available to you. It won't be what you do on the surface that is most interesting at the moment but rather the undertones of life. Does it seem as if almost every person you meet feels they are an expert in one thing or another? It's up to you to sort out the issues and decide on the best path.

21 TUESDAY ☿ *Moon Age Day 15   Moon Sign Gemini*

Now it pays great dividends to know what your competitors are up to. Getting ahead is all about being quite definite and making it plain what you want from life. Once you have laid your cards on the table you can afford to be slightly more aggressive in going for the prizes that seem to be on offer at present.

22 WEDNESDAY ☿ *Moon Age Day 16   Moon Sign Cancer*

Domestic issues can be unsettling now, particularly if everyone has a different idea about what to do. You may decide that calming everyone down and circumnavigating possible arguments is your job for today, especially where younger people are concerned. Make the most of some pleasant surprises that are available later.

23 THURSDAY ☿ *Moon Age Day 17   Moon Sign Cancer*

A boost to all family matters is now evident as the Sun moves into your solar fourth house. This is where it always resides at this time of year and it is one of the reasons you can excel at building a family Christmas. Even if you are late getting those final things done, you can still derive a great deal of joy from the most simple of duties.

24 FRIDAY ☿ *Moon Age Day 18   Moon Sign Leo*

Mercury is still in your solar third house and that fact adds to the social impulses that are presently so important. A string of new social contacts becomes possible and you may have a chance to get to know someone far better than you did before. Romantic impulses are positive for Christmas Eve, but Santa is on his way, so get everything organised!

25 SATURDAY ☿ *Moon Age Day 19   Moon Sign Leo*

An extra pleasant surprise could be the order of the day, over and above those that naturally come with the opening of presents. You can also take advantage of some family news and the opportunity to celebrate with friends. Whatever you get up to today, there's nothing wrong with being master of ceremonies.

26 SUNDAY ☿ *Moon Age Day 20   Moon Sign Virgo*

Some impatience is possible because in addition to having a fourth-house Sun you are also slightly troubled by the fact that fiery Mars is in the same part of your horoscope. This could bring frustration regarding some unbidden situations, so be prepared to deal with this eventuality.

27 MONDAY ☿ *Moon Age Day 21   Moon Sign Virgo*

This is a time of discrimination and self-examination, probably to a greater degree than is strictly necessary. Even if you don't get everything done that you had planned, on the way you can discover something new and interesting about yourself.

28 TUESDAY ☿ *Moon Age Day 22   Moon Sign Libra*

The Moon moves into Libra, giving you all the benefits of the lunar high at the very end of the year. Social impulses are to the fore, and you should have sufficient energy to move around freely and to involve yourself fully in life.

29 WEDNESDAY ☿ *Moon Age Day 23   Moon Sign Libra*

An ideal time to turn changes you want to make at home into more of a reality, and you are in a good position to influence the thinking of people who can be quite intransigent on occasions. Lady Luck encourages you to act as boldly as possible.

30 THURSDAY ☿ *Moon Age Day 24   Moon Sign Scorpio*

You may find yourself involved in a domestic situation that amounts to a clash of wills, but as the saying goes, there is more than one way to skin a cat. Use your very positive communication skills to address tricky issues and persuade others to behave.

31 FRIDAY *Moon Age Day 25   Moon Sign Scorpio*

The focus remains on communication, and you may well be extremely busy today, running from one situation to another. There are new ideas available at all stages, and these assist you to achieve a very positive start to the New Year.

RISING SIGNS FOR LIBRA

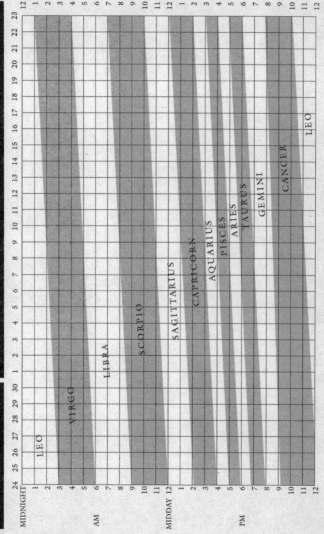

THE ZODIAC, PLANETS AND CORRESPONDENCES

The Earth revolves around the Sun once every calendar year, so when viewed from Earth the Sun appears in a different part of the sky as the year progresses. In astrology, these parts of the sky are divided into the signs of the zodiac and this means that the signs are organised in a circle. The circle begins with Aries and ends with Pisces.

Taking the zodiac sign as a starting point, astrologers then work with all the positions of planets, stars and many other factors to calculate horoscopes and birth charts and tell us what the stars have in store for us.

The table below shows the planets and Elements for each of the signs of the zodiac. Each sign belongs to one of the four Elements: Fire, Air, Earth or Water. Fire signs are creative and enthusiastic; Air signs are mentally active and thoughtful; Earth signs are constructive and practical; Water signs are emotional and have strong feelings.

It also shows the metals and gemstones associated with, or corresponding with, each sign. The correspondence is made when a metal or stone possesses properties that are held in common with a particular sign of the zodiac.

Finally, the table shows the opposite of each star sign – this is the opposite sign in the astrological circle.

Placed	Sign	Symbol	Element	Planet	Metal	Stone	Opposite
1	Aries	Ram	Fire	Mars	Iron	Bloodstone	Libra
2	Taurus	Bull	Earth	Venus	Copper	Sapphire	Scorpio
3	Gemini	Twins	Air	Mercury	Mercury	Tiger's Eye	Sagittarius
4	Cancer	Crab	Water	Moon	Silver	Pearl	Capricorn
5	Leo	Lion	Fire	Sun	Gold	Ruby	Aquarius
6	Virgo	Maiden	Earth	Mercury	Mercury	Sardonyx	Pisces
7	Libra	Scales	Air	Venus	Copper	Sapphire	Aries
8	Scorpio	Scorpion	Water	Pluto	Plutonium	Jasper	Taurus
9	Sagittarius	Archer	Fire	Jupiter	Tin	Topaz	Gemini
10	Capricorn	Goat	Earth	Saturn	Lead	Black Onyx	Cancer
11	Aquarius	Waterbearer	Air	Uranus	Uranium	Amethyst	Leo
12	Pisces	Fishes	Water	Neptune	Tin	Moonstone	Virgo